SPIRULINA
Nature's Superfood

By Kelly Moorhead and Bob Capelli
with Dr. Gerald R. Cysewski

Published by Cyanotech Corporation
Copyright 1993 by Cyanotech Corporation
Second printing 1995
Third printing 1996
Fourth printing 1998
Fifth printing 2001

2nd edition Copyright 2006 by Cyanotech Corporation
Second printing 2007
Third printing 2008
Fourth printing 2009

Publisher's Note

The information presented here is for educational purposes only. It is not to be taken as medical advice or as an attempt to sell a particular product. The opinions and beliefs expressed are those of the authors. People with medical problems or questions should consult a health professional. Information in this book is not intended to diagnose, treat, cure or prevent any disease.

This book may not be reproduced in whole or in part, by any means, without permission from Cyanotech Corporation, 73-4460 Queen Kaahumanu Hwy #102, Kailua-Kona, HI 96740.

Special thanks to Nicholle Davis for her diligent work in helping to prepare this book.

Front cover photo: Aerial view of microalgae farm of Cyanotech Corporation, Kailua-Kona, Hawaii.

ISBN 0-9637511-3-1

Table of Contents

Introduction [to the first edition, 1993]

In the tradition of the Aztecs, Mayas, Toltecs, Kanembu of Lake Chad, and other ancient cultures, the world is slowly coming back to a very basic approach to feeding itself: Eating low on the food chain by consuming nutrient rich microalgae, such as Spirulina. Excessive population growth, the contamination of our environment, and the decreased nutritive value of the food we eat has forced us, as individuals and as a world family, to seek alternatives to the packaged, processed, adulterated, overpriced foods that are sold everywhere. Simple, clean foods that can help us cope with the ever increasing psychological, emotional, and physical demands of twentieth century living are widely needed throughout the developing and industrialized world to keep us healthy and to keep us alive.

Though many reports are anecdotal, dietary supplementation with Spirulina and other microalgae may benefit diseases such as gastrointestinal ulcers, arthritis, allergies, diabetes, obesity, and hypertension. In searching for ways to truly reduce our national medical care expenditures, the Clinton Administration's Health Task Force would be wise to examine those community-based health education programs that can cost-effectively reverse the deterioration of the American diet and improve Americans' health.

Cyanotech Corporation in Kailua-Kona, Hawaii, arguably the world's foremost producer of impeccably pure Spirulina, has provided us with an invaluable service by introducing basic biochemical, nutritional, technological, medical, and supportive information about Spirulina. Through this book, consumers can now make more informed choices about the use of Spirulina in their own diets.

We on the Big Island of Hawaii are very proud of Cyanotech's contribution to the greening of our local island economy; the support their work gives to the notion of Hawaii, The Health State; and their commitment to education, scientific innovation, and microalgae research. This commitment is certain to benefit people worldwide.

Raymond Rosenthal, M.D.
Kailua-Kona, Hawaii

Spirulina — Superfood

Spirulina is a "Superfood." It is the most nutritious, concentrated whole food known to humankind. It has a rich, vibrant history, and occupies an intriguing biological and ecological niche in the plant kingdom. Spirulina is truly an amazing food, full of nutritional wonders.

Imagine a food that can help regulate blood sugar, blood pressure and cholesterol; a food that can alleviate pain from inflammation and deliver antioxidant activity to ward off life threatening diseases like cancer, Alzheimer's, heart disease and stroke; a food that helps and protects the liver and kidneys and removes radiation from the body; a food that improves the immune system, alleviates allergies and has been proven to fight many different viruses; a food that helps your eyes and brain; a food that can actually help you lose weight, increase friendly flora in the intestines and improve digestion. Scientific research shows that Spirulina may help in all of these areas and more. Don't believe it? This short book will tell you all about the scientific experiments and clinical trials that have shown these positive benefits. But the best way to find out for yourself is to try a bottle of Spirulina tablets or powder and see what it can do for you.

Spirulina's concentrated nutrition makes it an ideal food supplement for people of all ages and lifestyles. Spirulina is about sixty percent complete, highly digestible protein. Spirulina contains every essential amino acid. It contains more beta-carotene than any other whole food; it is the best whole food source of gamma linolenic acid (GLA); it is rich in B vitamins, minerals, trace elements, chlorophyll, and enzymes; and it is abundant in other valuable nutrients about which scientists are learning more each year, such as carotenoids, sulfolipids, glycolipids, phycocyanin, superoxide dismutase, RNA, and DNA.

Spirulina supplies nutrients that are lacking in most of our diets. It provides athletes with long-lasting energy and reduces recovery time; it nourishes people who have digestion, assimilation, and elimination problems; it satisfies the appetite as it provides essential nutrients to weight watchers; it enables children and others who don't like vegetables to eat their greens by taking a few tablets; and it helps busy people who don't have time for regular, balanced meals to nourish themselves. People with various health problems swear by Spirulina - it appears to promote overall health and well-being.

Comparing Spirulina with other foods shows just how packed it is with nutrients:

- Spirulina has 300% more calcium than whole milk
- Spirulina has 2300% more iron than spinach
- Spirulina has 3900% more beta carotene than carrots

- Spirulina has 375% more protein than tofu
- Three grams of Spirulina have more antioxidant and anti-inflammatory activity than five servings of vegetables
- Comparing phytonutrient levels, Spirulina is 31 times more potent than blueberries, 60 times more potent than spinach and 700 times more potent than apples

Algae – Our Benefactors

Algae were the first plants to appear on the planet. Billions of years ago, they transformed the carbon-dioxide-based atmosphere to an oxygen-rich atmosphere in which other life forms could evolve.

Most people think of algae as green or red stuff growing in the ocean or lakes, but, like land plants, there are countless different species of algae; algae come in different colors and sizes and provide everything from deadly toxins to potent medicines.

Of the more than 30,000 species of algae, blue-green algae, such as Spirulina, are the most primitive. They contain no nucleus and their cell walls are soft and easily digested, unlike those of other plants that contain hard cellulose. Of all the algae, Spirulina has emerged as the most potent and nutritious food. In fact, Spirulina is the most concentrated and nutritious whole food known to science. Although Spirulina has been around for millions of years, its widespread popularity as a food is very recent.

Natural Versus Processed

The health and fitness revolution has brought about new attitudes to diet and lifestyle. Now that we live longer, we want to stay strong and healthy. The demand for natural unprocessed food is growing daily. But, because most of us lead such busy lives, we need to prepare a lot of our meals in a hurry. We want our food to be fast and healthy – not just fast. We often eat out, and those meals are generally lower in nutrients than meals prepared at home.

The National Research Council's Committee on Diet and Health recommends that we eat 5-9 servings of fruit and vegetables a day; even for people who try to eat well, that's quite a challenge. Many of us don't make it a priority to prepare healthy meals every day. It's good to know that by eating just 3 grams of Spirulina each day we get more antioxidant and anti-inflammatory nutrients than are found in 5 servings of vegetables!

To remedy poor diets, many people take food supplements. Taking synthetic vitamin supplements can help; however good synthetics may be, natural food is always better. The body absorbs and utilizes food more efficiently than it does synthetics. Intuitively our bodies prefer food, and Spirulina is an extremely digestible, nutritious food.

Nutrition for People of All Ages

Spirulina is a perfect complimentary nutrient for people of all ages. No RDAs (Recommended Daily Allowances) have been set for the elderly, but their nutritional needs are different from those of other age groups. They are more likely than younger people to be deficient in certain nutrients and may not absorb, utilize, or store nutrients efficiently. Many elderly people are on medication for extended periods, which interferes with nutrient levels. It may not be easy to obtain all the required nutrients from food, so it is important to take food supplements that can be easily digested and utilized by the body. Spirulina is a high-energy food, and due to its soft cell wall, Spirulina offers nutrients in an easily assimilable form. People of all ages also take Spirulina for its cleansing effect and its ability to help improve digestion and elimination.

The amount of Spirulina taken can be adjusted to fit the needs of an individual according to their age, health status or the particular results they want to achieve. Children who won't eat their vegetables and students away from home should take Spirulina. People who do not consistently eat good, nutritious food are also good candidates for Spirulina. Older people and people recovering from operations should take Spirulina. People who need more energy or aren't eating a well balanced diet should take Spirulina; in fact, all of the groups mentioned above should eat Spirulina every day.

It's reassuring to know that, even when we're busy, with not enough time to shop or cook, we can still eat our greens by taking Spirulina. We're not suggesting that taking Spirulina makes it all right to live on junk food, but Spirulina is certainly a good addition to any diet.

Pets and Plants

Spirulina is not only good for people: Animals and plants thrive on it too. When given Spirulina, old cats and dogs with dull, thinning coats have been seen to develop thick, lustrous coats; and pets with stiff joints appear to improve considerably, becoming supple and active again.

Veterinarians prescribe Spirulina to aid recovery, increase stamina, relieve stiffness, and also for show animals for general toning, as these animals need to look their best.

Prize winning koi carp are fed Spirulina to enhance their color and health. Bird breeders add Spirulina to feed to enhance plumage color and luster. Spirulina is used extensively by aquaculture companies to improve the growth rates, increase disease resistance, improve survival rates, reduce medication requirements and improve quality and coloration of various fish and shellfish (Henson 1990).

Gardeners can use Spirulina as a complete, effective foliar plant food. Homeowners can sprinkle a little Spirulina in the earth around their favorite houseplant and see what a difference it makes. Organic farmers can use Spirulina as a completely natural and healthy fertilizer. In one case, an organic lettuce grower in Hawaii saw a tremendous increase in the yield and health of his lettuce by fertilizing with Spirulina, while a farmer across the street using conventional fertilizer had lettuce that grew much slower and smaller.

Complete Protein

Spirulina is about sixty percent protein - far more than any other food. Its protein is complete, meaning that it contains all the essential amino acids. While most animal proteins are high in fat, calories, and cholesterol, Spirulina is only five percent fat, most of which is beneficial unsaturated fatty acids like GLA (more on this wonderful nutrient later). There are less than four calories in each gram and practically no cholesterol.

Spirulina's protein is easily digested and assimilated. Other plants have cell walls of hard, indigestible cellulose, while Spirulina's cell walls consist of soft mucopolysaccharides, making it easy for the body to digest. Digestibility and absorption are very important factors, especially for undernourished people, convalescents, and the elderly.

To determine the percentage of usable protein in a food, we measure the amount of protein present, its digestibility, and its biological value. The only food with more usable protein than Spirulina is eggs. None of the protein sources in the chart below has even close to the amount of other nutrients that Spirulina has; and of course, many of these other protein sources have very negative properties as well, such as animal fat and cholesterol.

Usable Protein Of Common Protein Foods *

Food	Protein (%)	NPU (%)**	Usable Protein (%)
Dried eggs	47	94	44
Spirulina	65	57	37
Dried skimmed milk	36	82	30
Soy flour	37	61	23
Fish	22	80	18
Chicken	24	67	16
Beef	22	67	16
Peanuts	26	38	10

* Switzer (1982)   ** Net Protein Utilization

The Case for Dietary Antioxidants

For most people the term oxygen has pleasant connotations. From the healing air in a forest to the serenity gained from deep breathing, oxygen is very soothing. As is typical in nature, however, there are positive and negative aspects of oxygen. Although oxygen is essential for metabolism, it is a very reactive compound. Sometimes oxygen will combine with the complex molecules of metabolism to make reactive intermediate compounds which can be dangerous.

Free Radicals

When oxygen combines with the complex metabolic molecules it creates compounds called free radicals. Small quantities of free radicals are produced during normal body metabolism, such as breathing and digestion. Exposure to sunlight and bacterial infections promotes free radical formation. Athletes tend to generate more free radicals during strenuous exercise, when they burn more of the body's fuel. Large quantities are present in many of the pollutants our bodies are exposed to, like smoke, burnt food, car exhaust, and many chemicals. Free radicals are highly unstable molecules ready to react (oxidize) with anything. Once free radicals are formed, they can trigger a chain reaction that produces other free radicals. The human body produces some antioxidants like superoxide dismutase to help alleviate the free radicals produced by the body; unfortunately, living in today's world with higher stress levels, pollution and mass-produced foods increases our bodies' free radical levels above what can be eliminated by the antioxidants produced by the body.

The outward manifestations of free radical damage are lines, wrinkles, dry skin, loss of muscle tone, and even skin cancer. Internally, free radicals impair immune function, damage tissue, and generally weaken or destroy cells. Damage to cells includes the DNA; and damage to the DNA of our cells is now thought to be a major component of the aging process. DNA contains the cells' instructions for when to divide, how to make enzymes and other proteins, and how to direct all the other cellular activities. Once this "blueprint" has been damaged, cells lose their ability to function normally. Damage to DNA is usually repaired, but occasionally the repair job is defective. In the worst case, a cancerous cell line can begin. Fortunately, we have immune systems that are generally, but not always, capable of detecting and eliminating cancerous cells. But of course, it is better to avoid this last line of defense and prevent the damage in the first place.

Antioxidants

An antioxidant is capable of joining with a free radical and rendering it harmless. One can visualize a free radical as a spilled liquid and the antioxidant as the sponge. When antioxidants are present, the cell can proceed with its business without damage. Certain natural foods and herbs are the source of most antioxidants, which is why diet is so important in maintaining a healthy and strong body and a cancer-preventive lifestyle. Besides quitting or avoiding smoking, modifying your diet is the single most important factor in cancer avoidance. Eating foods rich in antioxidants such as carotenoids, phycocyanin, superoxide dismutase and vitamins C and E is another great way to help prevent cancer.

Carotenoids

Carotenoids are vitally important antioxidants. Numerous studies have indicated that people whose diets contain a lot of foods rich in carotenoids lower their risk of developing various types of cancer (see the section on Scientific Research).

Natural vs. synthetic: A good illustration of the importance of taking natural vitamins from food can be made with beta-carotene, one of the carotenoids present in Spirulina in large quantities. There are many synthetic beta-carotene supplements on the market. In fact, even some that claim to be "natural" are synthetic. Nature makes beta-carotene in two shapes, called cis and trans, while synthetic is primarily only one shape (trans). The two forms of beta-carotene are displayed in the following diagram.

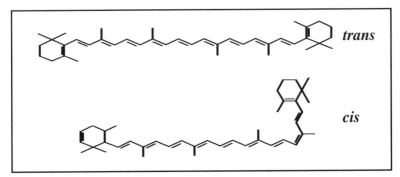

Molecular structure of nature's two forms of beta-carotene. Synthetic is only the trans form.

Cis and trans forms of beta-carotene are two different compounds, different chemically, and different physically. They behave differently when crystallizing and when dissolving. There is also a difference when they are absorbed in the intestine for digestion. In fact, a study showed that chickens and rats

7

absorb ten times more natural beta-carotene than synthetic! In studies where beta-carotene is correlated with lower incidence of cancer, the beta-carotene is from natural food. This is one reason why major government agencies, such as the National Institute of Health and the National Cancer Institute, recommend natural food sources of beta-carotene.

Another advantage of natural beta-carotene is that it contains no artificial ingredients or preservatives, whereas synthetic beta-carotene contains preservatives and trace residues of chemicals used in the refining process.

There are between 400 and 600 carotenoids about which we know very little: Almost all the research so far has concentrated on beta-carotene, lutein, lycopene, zeaxanthin and most recently astaxanthin. The full range of carotenoids is only found in food, which is why it is important to include carotenoid-rich foods in our diet.

It is quite possible that the other carotenoids are just as valuable for our health as beta-carotene. Carotenoids are used and stored in several parts of the body, including the adrenal glands, the reproductive system, the pancreas and spleen, the skin, and the retina. Depletion of these stores results in disturbances in the body despite adequate levels of beta-carotene in one's diet.

Sources of Natural Beta-carotene

There are many food sources of beta-carotene. Spinach and kale and other dark green leafy vegetables, broccoli, pumpkin, carrots, squash, papayas, cantaloupes, and other yellow and orange fruits and vegetables are all excellent sources. Regrettably, however, most people get only 25-30% of the daily dietary carotenoid intake recommended in a cancer-preventive diet; and many people are unwilling to make radical dietary changes.

The easy way to eat your daily dose of food-based beta-carotene is to take Spirulina, the richest whole food source of beta-carotene. Unlike other beta-carotene supplements, Spirulina is a whole food with its beta-carotene in a naturally chelated food matrix. And Spirulina is not only rich in beta-carotene, it contains other very important carotenoids like zeaxanthin and beta-cryptoxanthin as well as lesser known carotenoids such as myxoxanthophyll and echinenone.

Food Comparison Chart

Food	Beta-carotene
Hawaiian Spirulina*, 3 grams	9.0 mg
Carrot, 1 medium	4.9 mg
Papaya, 1 medium	3.7 mg
Chlorella, 3 grams	1.0 mg
Apricot, 1 medium	0.9 mg

*From Cyanotech Corporation

Dosage and Timing

How much Spirulina should you take, and when? As a dietary supplement, the recommended minimum amount is three grams daily – one teaspoon of powder or six 500 mg tablets. Since it is a pure and natural food, you may safely take more, to suit your personal health program.

Because high-protein foods have been found to increase alertness – and Spirulina is the richest whole food source of protein – it is best to take Spirulina at least four hours before going to bed. Otherwise, you can take it whenever you like – with, before, or between meals; before or after working out; or whenever your energy level is low. People often ask whether they should take all six tablets at once or take two tablets three times a day. The answer is, it really doesn't seem to matter. People report feeling benefits whenever and however they take Spirulina. And since many of the nutrients in Spirulina are not water soluble and are thus not eliminated from the body by urination, taking all your Spirulina at once rather than throughout the day does not present any problems.

Many people are so used to taking synthetic supplements that they are shocked at the idea of taking ten, twenty or thirty tablets a day. However, if you think of it as eating a snack or part of a meal, then ten or twenty grams is not excessive. Body builders and other athletes often eat as much as fifty grams a

Typical Analysis of Hawaiian Spirulina[*]

(Typical Analysis per 3 grams – one teaspoon or six 500mg tablets)

General Composition

Protein	53-62%
Carbohydrates	17-25%
Lipids	4-6%
Minerals	8-13%
Moisture	3-6%

Minerals

Calcium	14 mg
Magnesium	23.mg
Iron	1.6 mg
Phosphorus	30 mg
Potassium	56 mg
Sodium	42 mg
Manganese	96 mcg
Zinc	81 mcg
Boron	90 mcg
Copper	21 mcg
Molybdenum	12 mcg
Selenium	1.0 mcg

Vitamins

Vitamin A (100% as Beta-Carotene)	11,250 IU
Vitamin B1 Thiamine	75 mcg
Vitamin B2 Riboflavin	110 mcg
Vitamin B3 Niacin	450 mcg
Vitamin B6	15 mcg
Human Active B12 (Cobalamin)**	2.0 mcg
Vitamin E (d-a tocopherol)	45 mcg
Inositol	1.7 mcg
Biotin	0.8 mcg
Folic Acid	4.5 mcg
Pantothenic Acid	4.5 mcg

Phytonutrients

Beta-Carotine	9mg
Chlorophyll	24 mg
Total Carotenoids	13 mg
Phycocyanin	360 mg
Superoxide Dismutase	2250 units

Spirulina is also a rich source of enzymes, RNA, DNA, sulfolipids, glycogen, and other potentially important nutrients.

*Hawaiian Spirulina grown by Cyanotech Corporation on the Kona Coast
**Standard reporting methods list total corrinoid B12. However , we would like you to know the actual amount of B12 that is bioavailable to humans.

Fatty Acids (Total 48 mg per gram)

Omega 6 Family

Gamma Linolenic (GLA)	30 mg
Essential Linoleic	33 mg
Dihomogamma Linolenic	1.59 mg

Omega 3 Family

Alpha Linolenic	0.0435 mg
Docosahexaenoic (DHA)	0.0435 mg

Monoenoic Family

Palmitoleic	5.94 mg
Oleic	0.51 mg
Erucic	0.072 mg

Other Fatty Acids

Palmitic Acid	61 mg
Myristic acid	0.4 mg
Stearic Acid	2.5 mg
Arachidonic	0.2 mg
Behenic Acid	0.144 mg
Lignoceric Acid	0.072 mg

Protein

Spirulina is a superior source of dietary protein – up to 60% highly digestible protein, containing all essential amino acids.

Typical Amino Acid Analysis

Essential amino Acids	% of Total	Mg per Gram
Isoleucine	5.43	32.6
Leucine	8.15	48.9
Lysine	4.37	26.2
Methionine	2.22	13.3
Phenylalanine	4.35	26.1
Threonine	4.68	28.1
Tryptophan	1.41	8.5
Valine	6.23	37.4
Non-Essential amino Acids		
Alanine	7.74	46.6
Arginine	7.94	47.6
Aspartic Acid	12.14	72.8
Cystine	0.93	5.6
Glutamic Acid	14.07	84.4
Glycine	5.32	31.9
Histidine	2.50	15.0
Proline	4.11	24.7
Serine	4.42	26.5
Tyrosine	3.97	23.8
Total	**100.0**	**600.0**

day. Many people get great results by varying the amount they take. For example, if you are under a lot of stress, working long hours, or using a lot of physical energy, you may wish to increase your dose. Weight watchers may like to experiment until they find the optimum amount that helps to satisfy their appetites.

It is important to note that Spirulina is a natural cleanser and helps to eliminate toxins from the body, especially when it is first taken. A few people, (approximately 1 – 2%) may experience slight changes in there digestive systems for the first few days when taking Spirulina. These changes are always short-lived, and after a few days these people are back to normal and usually report feeling better than ever due to all the positive benefits of Spirulina.

Medical Research

Some of the nutrients in Spirulina, such as superoxide dismutase, glycolipids, sulfolipids, various carotenoids, RNA, and DNA, are just beginning to receive attention, while others have yet to be researched, and it will be many years before we have enough scientific data to draw conclusions about their contribution to our wellbeing. For example, we still know relatively little about the trace elements and the more than 2000 enzymes in Spirulina; but researchers have been studying Spirulina for over thirty years now and a great deal has been proven about the many benefits of Spirulina consumption.

The National Research Council makes dietary recommendations based on foods rather than on specific nutrients contained in those foods. Absolute scientific proof of the benefits of certain nutrients is hard to obtain, and many more years of rigorous testing are needed to verify current dietary theories. The general effects of a type of diet are easier to ascertain. For example, we now know that high-fat diets are linked to some types of cancer. Researchers have estimated that approximately 35% of all deaths from cancer are related to diet (Doll and Pete 1981), and the figure could be as high as 70%. Wynder and Gori (1979) estimated that 40% of cancer incidence among men and almost 60% among women is related to diet. Eating a diet rich in vegetables and fruit is an excellent way to decrease your risk of cancer, heart disease and other life threatening illnesses. Eating Spirulina every day is another important step you can take to live a long and healthy life.

Spirulina Research

There have been over 200 scientific studies including in-vitro experiments, in-vivo animal research and double blind, placebo-controlled human clinical trials that have showed a vast array of positive health benefits from Spirulina. In the interest of brevity we will examine just a fraction of these studies here.

An excellent summary study of Spirulina was done in 2002. The authors summarized the many potential benefits of Spirulina: "Spirulina has been experimentally proven, in vivo and in vitro that it is effective to treat **certain allergies, anemia, cancer, hepatotoxicity [toxicity of the liver], viral and cardiovascular diseases, hyperglycemia [high blood sugar], hyperlipidemia [high cholesterol and triglycerides], immunodeficiency, and inflammatory processes**, among others. Several of these activities are attributed to Spirulina itself or to some of its components including fatty acids omega-3 or omega-6, beta-carotene, alpha-tocopherol, phycocyanin, phenol compounds and a recently isolated complex, Calcium Spirulan." (Chamorro et al, 2002)

Another summary study in 2001 analyzed some of the benefits mentioned above as well as some additional potential benefits. The authors pointed out that Spirulina was proven to stimulate the **immune system** and augment **resistance** in humans as well as animals (including mammals, poultry and fish) by stimulating the production of antibodies and cytokines. It went on to point out that "Spirulina sulfolipids have proved to be effective against **HIV**. Preparations obtained from Spirulina biomass have also been found active against **herpes** virus, **cytomegalovirus**, **influenza** virus, etc. Spirulina extracts are capable in inhibiting **carcinogenesis [production of cancer]**." The study went on to point out that Spirulina is also effective in preserving **intestinal flora** and in decreasing **Candida albicans (yeast infections)**. (Blinkova et al, 2001)

The reference above to Spirulina's effectiveness with **HIV** is very interesting, and a very recent study done at the University of South Carolina focused on this topic. This study is titled "Algae—a poor man's HAART" (HIV/AIDS anti-retroviral therapy). This study examines the in vivo and in vitro HIV inhibition by algae, and goes on to point out that the people of Chad including the Kanembu tribe who eat Spirulina daily have a much lower incidence of HIV/AIDS than Africans in surrounding countries, which cannot be explained by differences in sexual behavior or intravenous drug use. The study hypothesizes that "regular consumption of dietary algae might help prevent HIV infection and suppress viral load among those infected." (Teas et al, 2004)

Previously, scientists at the prestigious Harvard Medical School in

Boston found that a water extract of Spirulina prevented the replication of **HIV-1** virus in human T-cell lines. The viral production was reduced by approximately 50%. The researchers separated the extract into a polysaccharide fraction and a fraction depleted of polysaccharides and found antiviral activity in both. They concluded that the water extracts of Spirulina "contain antiretroviral activity that may be of potential clinical interest" (Ayehunie et al, 1998).

A very important clinical trial was done on tobacco chewers that had **pre-cancerous** lesions in their mouths. The group taking Spirulina (at a remarkably low dose of only one gram per day) had complete regression of the lesions in 20 of 44 cases (45%). In the placebo group, only 3 of 43 (7%) showed regression. Within one year of discontinuing Spirulina consumption 9 out of 20 (45%) of the subjects that had complete regression developed new lesions! (Mathew et al, 1995)

In a study done in Europe that examined the effect that Spirulina has on patients with **multiple sclerosis**, the researchers said "It has been established that intake of Spirulina makes for lengthening of remission in those patients with disseminated sclerosis (Buletsa et al, 1996).

Spirulina has been shown to help the **liver** and to help people already suffering from **liver disease**. A study was done on 60 patients with chronic diffuse disorders of the liver as well as 70 animals with toxic affection of the liver. They found that Spirulina was effective for both the people and the animals. They attributed the hepatoprotective (liver-protecting) properties of Spirulina to its anti-inflammatory, antioxidant, membrane-stabilizing and immunocorrecting actions. They found that Spirulina stabilized the liver disease and prevented the disease from progressing to cirrhosis (Gorban et al, 2000).

A recent study done at the University of California Davis's School of Medicine had allergy researchers examine Spirulina's effect on **allergic rhinitis (allergies that cause inflammation of the mucous membrane of the nose)**. The study proved that by using Spirulina patients reduced the cytokine Interleukin-4 and the researchers concluded that Spirulina demonstrates protective effects on sufferers of allergic rhinitis (Mao et al, 2005).

Countless animal studies have shown positive benefits from Spirulina consumption. A study done on rats showed excellent prospects for Spirulina as a **neuroprotective** supplement. The study proved that Spirulina reduced ischemic **brain damage** in rats, and that these rats had **improved post-stroke locomotor activity** (Wang et al, 2005). The same researchers had previously demonstrated that Spirulina reduces **degeneration of the brain** of aged animals. Another group which measured oxidative damage found similar results in aged rats' brains. Spirulina decreased the oxidation in the brain and also decreased pro-inflammatory cytokines (Gemma et al, 2002). A study of cats found that Spirulina may improve **disease resistance** (Qureshi and Ali, 1996). Spirulina was also found to increase several different **immunological functions** in chickens (Qureshi et al, 1996). A study in mice in Japan found similar results: Spirulina enhanced **immune response** through multiple pathways (Hayashi et al, 1994). Another mouse study showed that Spirulina reduced both **skin and stomach tumors** significantly. Spirulina was shown to reduce both the size of the tumors and to reduce the incidence of tumors (Dasgupta et al, 2001).

Diabetic mice showed very positive results when given Spirulina in one study which led the researchers to conclude that "It is worth future work of Spirulina on humans looking for better quality of life and longer survival of diabetic patients (Rodriguez et al, 2001). Rats with **high blood lipid levels** showed improvement when fed Spirulina (Iwata et al, 1990). Spirulina also was shown to dose-dependently reduce **allergic reactions** in rats (Kim et al, 1998).

Other animal studies have shown very diverse results. Spirulina was shown to prevent **fatty liver development** in rats (Torres et al, 1998). Spirulina was also shown to significantly increase **iron storage and hemoglobin blood counts** in pregnant and lactating rats (Kapoor and Mehta, 1998). The same researchers found earlier that Spirulina-fed rats showed **faster growth rates** than rats fed a standard diet without Spirulina. They also showed that Spirulina **increased the litter size** of pregnant rats and concluded that "Spirulina appears to be a **good dietary supplement during pregnancy**" (Kapoor and Mehta, 1993).

In earlier human research, Spirulina has been observed to assist in the **treatment of wounds** (Clement et al 1967) and to lower cholesterol (Nayaka et al 1988). Groups of **undernourished children and adults** have responded well to being fed Spirulina (Sautier and Tremolieres 1976).

Carotenoids

The National Research Council and other research organizations recommend that we eat at least 5 – 9 servings of fruits and vegetables each day, especially green and yellow vegetables and citrus fruits, because of the link between eating them and decreased susceptibility to some cancers (National Research Council 1989). There is strong evidence that it is the carotenoids and antioxidants in these foods that offer protection against **cancer**. Unfortunately, most of us do not eat the recommended 5 – 9 servings. This is where the great advantage of Spirulina lies: it is a carotenoid rich food—the richest—and it can be taken in tablet or powder form to supplement our diets.

Spirulina and its individual nutrients are receiving a lot of attention from the scientific community. Carotenoids are rapidly becoming known as the superstars of nutrition as more people realize that antioxidants play a vital role in human health. "The consumption of a diet rich in carotenoids has been epidemiologically correlated with a **lower risk for several diseases**." (Stahl and Sies, 2005) Scientists in Australia recently found that **prostate cancer risk** declined with increasing consumption of carotenoids including lycopene, lutein, alpha-carotene, beta-carotene, beta-cryptoxanthin and zeaxanthin (the latter three out of the six listed are present in Spirulina). They concluded that diets containing carotenoid-rich fruits and vegetables may be protective against prostate cancer. (Jian et al, 2005) Many earlier studies have found similar relationships between carotenoid intake and other forms of **cancer**.

Beta-Carotene

Some astonishing work with carotenoids is showing that they may be much more than free radical absorbers. Leading edge researchers have discovered that some carotenoids actually affect **the way our cells communicate**. For example, **cancerous cell lines** are typically unable to receive growth-controlling chemical signals from other cells. Beta-carotene opens the membrane communication channels of cancerous and pre-cancerous cells, allowing the body to signal the cancerous line to stop dividing. Thus, foods rich in carotenoids, in this case beta-carotene, may not only be able to prevent but also **reverse cancers** (Wolf 1992).

Another study showed that beta-carotene reduces the size of **tumors** that were already present in hamsters and slowed new tumor growth, extending the hamsters' survival time (Schwartz et al 1988).

Beta-carotene also has all the benefits of vitamin A. Our bodies make vitamin A out of beta-carotene, but with beta-carotene there is no risk of vitamin A toxicity because the body will only convert as much beta-carotene to vitamin

16

A as it needs. Whereas prolonged use of large amounts of vitamin A can cause skin rashes, hair loss, headaches, and irreversible liver damage, no toxicity or side effects have been found even with very large doses of beta-carotene. Excess beta-carotene circulates in the blood and is stored in fat tissue: an orange tint to the skin, especially in the palms of the hands, indicates reserves of beta-carotene.

Natural beta-carotene is chemically and physically different from the synthetic form. And although there is evidence that **the body absorbs natural beta-carotene ten times more easily than it absorbs the synthetic** form (Ben-Amotz et al 1989), most controlled studies with beta-carotene use the synthetic form. However, since the studies are showing that synthetic beta-carotene appears to be helping to protect against cancer and heart disease, it would indeed be interesting to see the results of studies involving natural beta-carotene. One such study noted significant differences between the use of synthetic and dietary beta-carotene (Brevard 1989).

Numerous studies have shown that people whose diets are high in beta-carotene have a lower incidence of various cancers (Ziegler 1989). Smokers, who are especially vulnerable, should maintain their beta-carotene levels. Low beta-carotene levels in the blood of smokers have been connected with the later appearance of **lung cancer** (Stahelin et al 1991). Researchers at Albert Einstein College of Medicine have shown that beta-carotene exerts a protective effect against the development and progression of **cervical cancer** (Palan et al 1992). Beta-carotene may also help to **protect the skin** against the damaging effects of sunlight and help to prevent **skin cancers** (Kornhauser et al 1986).

In the early 1980's a landmark study by the US National Science Foundation entitled Diet, Nutrition and Cancer, concluded on the basis of epidemiological evidence that diets rich in beta carotene were correlated with a reduction in the incidence of **cancer**. In fact, over 200 studies of dietary consumption of beta-carotene indicated a reduction of a range of cancers. Subsequent to those results scientists began a very large clinical trial of heavy smokers (two packs or more per day) in Finland to determine if supplementation with synthetic beta carotene would reduce the incidence of cancer. (Remember, synthetic beta carotene is different than that found in Spirulina in that it contains only the all-trans (no bends) version of the molecule while natural sources like Spirulina provide several cis-forms (molecules that have bends in them) as well as the all-trans form.)

The results of the trial were surprising in that contrary to the hypothesis, the beta-carotene supplemented group had a small (statistically *insignificant*) increase in the incidence of lung cancer. Interestingly, the group in the study with the highest blood levels of beta carotene from _dietary_ sources had the lowest incidence of lung cancer.

Scientists theorized that these results came from the fact that beta-carotene works in combination with Vitamin C to reduce the energy of free radicals. In the absence of Vitamin C, beta-carotene can actually form a pro-oxidant, leading to accelerated tissue cellular damage. Because of the high intake of free radicals in the lungs by smokers, they become deficient in Vitamin C and this is thought to be the reason supplementing heavy smokers with beta-carotene can cause a slight increase in cancer risk. (Note: There are very few antioxidants that never become pro-oxidants. The only two well researched carotenoid antioxidants that never become pro-oxidants are astaxanthin and zeaxanthin. So if you smoke, be sure to take Spirulina for its natural beta-carotene and zeaxanthin carotenoid antioxidants, take a natural astaxanthin supplement and take some Vitamin C as well.)

One of the largest studies to determine the relationship between beta-carotene and cancers is the ten-year study at Harvard Medical School involving 22,000 physicians. An interim report concentrated on 333 of the doctors who were showing signs of **coronary artery disease** when the study began. Those who were taking the beta-carotene supplements suffered about half as many **heart attacks, strokes, heart surgeries**, and other major cardiovascular events as those taking a placebo. Although the study was intended to look at beta-carotene and cancer, results are showing that beta-carotene also plays a role in preventing heart disease. It appears to discourage the formation and oxidation of low-density lipoprotein (LDL) cholesterol, thus lessening the damage to arteries that results in **atherosclerosis** (Johns Hopkins University 1991). In a smaller study involving people who chew tobacco, results have shown that taking beta-carotene supplements reduces oral **precancerous lesions** (Stich et al 1991).

As we grow older, immunological functions decrease, and the body's repair system begins to fail, making us more susceptible to diseases and other health problems. Antioxidants, in particular carotenoids, help to prevent the free radical damage associated with the aging process itself.

There is strong evidence that beta-carotene also enhances many aspects of **immune function** (Bendich 1988). It stimulates immunocompetence in healthy individuals and enhances immune function in people who have tested **HIV** positive (Garewal et al 1992). The cells of the immune system are among the most sensitive to oxidation.

In other research, the severity of **measles** in children has been reduced with vitamin A supplementation; and children who suffered higher fevers and were hospitalized with measles were found to have low vitamin A levels (Frieden et al 1992). Measles is one of the severest infectious diseases in poor communities; and vitamin A given to children with complicated measles was seen to enhance **immune-competence and decrease morbidity and mortality** (Coutsoudis et al 1992).

Lastly, large doses of beta-carotene were given to people with a disorder called erythropoietic protoporphyria (EPP), which is a **hypersensitivity to visible light**. In several studies over three-quarters of the patients experienced significant improvement in their ability to tolerate exposure to light; and over three-quarters of those could now spend four times longer out in the sun (Mathews-Roth 1981). This was especially important to children who could now play outdoors. There is evidence that carotenoids also help protect against other forms of photosensitivity (Kornhauser et al 1986).

Zeaxanthin

The second most prevalent carotenoid in Spirulina is zeaxanthin. In fact, there is more zeaxanthin in just 3 grams of Hawaiian Spirulina than there is in a large bowl of spinach, one of nature's richest sources. Zeaxanthin is a very important antioxidant for two reasons: 1) It is one of the few antioxidants that can **cross the blood brain barrier** and bring antioxidant protection to the **eyes, brain and central nervous** system and 2) it is also one of the few antioxidants that **never becomes a pro-oxidant**. It's true that many wonderful antioxidants can become pro-oxidants (cause oxidation in the body) in the absence of sufficient supporting antioxidants. Zeaxanthin and astaxanthin are two carotenoids that never become pro-oxidants in any situation. These two facts about zeaxanthin are leading researchers to study zeaxanthin more and more, and as they do, they're finding out that it is a powerful antioxidant with many benefits. In the chart below, zeaxanthin beat out all other antioxidants tested except for astaxanthin in singlet oxygen quenching rates. It beat Vitamin E by over 400 times! (Please note that there are many different ways to measure antioxidant strength, and this is just one test.)

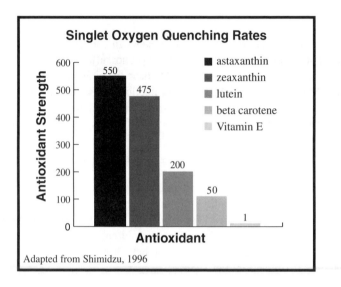

Singlet Oxygen Quenching Rates

- astaxanthin
- zeaxanthin
- lutein
- beta carotene
- Vitamin E

Antioxidant Strength

astaxanthin 550
zeaxanthin 475
lutein 200
beta carotene 50
Vitamin E 1

Antioxidant

Adapted from Shimidzu, 1996

An article in the June 2005 issue of the Alternative Medicine Review summarized some of the benefits of zeaxanthin and its closely related xanthophyll carotenoid lutein: "Lutein and zeaxanthin are the only carotenoids found in both the **macula and lens of the human eye**, and have dual functions in both tissues – to act as powerful antioxidants and to filter high-energy blue light…In addition to playing pivotal roles in ocular health, lutein and zeaxanthin are important nutrients for the prevention of **cardiovascular disease**, **stroke** and **lung cancer**. They may also be protective in **skin conditions** attributed to excessive ultraviolet (UV) light exposure."

Researchers at the Antioxidants Research Laboratory, a subsidiary of the United States Department of Agriculture's Human Nutrition Research Center on Aging, added to the above, citing zeaxanthin's potential role in the prevention of **cardiovascular** disease: "Epidemiological studies indicating an inverse relationship between xanthophylls [zeaxanthin is a xanthophyll] intake or status and both **cataract and age-related macular degeneration** suggest these compounds can play a protective role in the eye. Some observational studies have also shown these xanthophylls may help reduce the risk of certain types of **cancer**, particularly those of the breast and lung. Emerging studies suggest as well a potential contribution of lutein and zeaxanthin to the prevention of **heart disease and stroke**." (Ribaya-Mercado and Blumberg, 2004)

A study done in the Netherlands examined the role that zeaxanthin and beta-carotene had on **inflammation-caused atherosclerosis**. They found that the inverse relationship between these carotenoids and leukocytes may explain the possible protective effect of carotenoids on atherosclerosis through their work as anti-inflammatories (van Herpen-Broekmans et al, 2004).

Phycocyanin

Phycocyanin is being studied more and more by scientists in recent years. The word "phycocyanin" comes from the Greek word for algae "phyco" and the Greek word for blue "cyan." Phycocyanin is an amazing water-soluble blue pigment that gives Spirulina its bluish tint. Phycocyanin is only found in blue-green algae like Spirulina—you can't get it in other foods. Phycocyanin is one of the key ingredients that make Spirulina such a wonderful Superfood, and a vital difference between Spirulina and other green foods like chlorella, wheat grass and barley.

Phycocyanin is a powerful water soluble antioxidant. Scientists in Spain showed that an extract of Spirulina containing phycocyanin is a **potent free radical scavenger** and inhibits microsomal lipid peroxidation (Pinero et al, 2001). Spirulina has many different types of antioxidants, and the unique nature of phycocyanin makes Spirulina a level above other antioxidant foods or formulas. It is the phycocyanin in Spirulina that is thought to help protect against **renal (kidney) failure** caused by certain drug therapies administered in hospitals. Phycocyanin has also shown promise in treating **cancer** in animals and stimulating the **immune system** (Iijima et al 1982). A recent study showed that phycocyanin is a powerful **anti-inflammatory** (Reddy et al 2000). It has also been shown to inhibit the **allergic inflammatory response** (Ramirez et al 2002). Phycocyanin combats inflammation as a Cox-2 inhibitor. Prescription Cox-2 inhibitors can damage the liver, but phycocyanin actually helps the **liver**.

A great deal of research has been done in Japan on phycocyanin. The Japanese have found that phycocyanin **protects the liver and the kidneys during detoxification**, as well as activating the **immune system**. Researchers at the Osaka Medical Center for Cancer and Cardiovascular Diseases said "Spirulina is surmised to potentiate the **immune system** leading to suppression of **cancer development** and **viral infection**." Their human clinical study showed that a hot water extract of Spirulina rich in phycocyanin **increased interferon production** and NK cytotoxicity **(cancer killing cells)** when taken orally (Hirahashi et al, 2002).

21

Cuban scientists have also been looking at the many properties of phycocyanin. Animal studies done with rodents showed that phycocyanin has **anti-inflammatory activity due to prostaglandin E-2 inhibition** (Romay et al, 2000) and that it reduces **allergic inflammatory response and histamine release from cells** (Remirez et al, 2002).

Another study indicated that Spirulina had an **anti-arthritic** effect in mice, which they said may be due to the anti-inflammatory and antioxidant properties of phycocyanin (Remirez et al, 2002)

Another study in Cuba concluded that phycocyanin has **antioxidant, anti-inflammatory, neuroprotective (brain) and hepatoprotective (liver) effects** (Romay et al 2003). Their work was done both in-vitro and in-vivo. In twelve experimental modules of inflammation, phycocyanin exerted a dose-dependant anti-inflammatory effect in every case. These scientists also found that phycocyanin reduced levels of tumor necrosis factor in mice and showed neuroprotective effects in rats.

An interesting study was done in Ukraine (where Spirulina had previously shown effectiveness in removing **radioactivity** from the urine of children suffering from high levels of radiation from the Chernobyl nuclear accident). This study was done with rats that were exposed to x-rays. The study found that rats fed phycocyanin experienced a correcting effect of the radiation exposure (Karpov et al, 2000).

Similar to studies done on Spirulina in its entirety, water extracts of Spirulina that are rich in phycocyanin have shown excellent **antiviral** properties. In one such experiment done at the National School of Biological Sciences in Mexico City the phycocyanin-rich extract inhibited the infection for **herpes simplex virus 1 and 2, pseudo-rabies virus and human cytomegalovirus** (Hernandez-Corona et al, 2002). In another study, a Spirulina water extract was compared with a chlorella water extract. Since chlorella has no phycocyanin, it performed much worse than Spirulina in relation to **liver disease** cells. The extracts of these two algae both showed positive effects, but Spirulina had a stronger effect than chlorella. The researcher pointed out, "the growth inhibitory effects of aqueous Spirulina extract on human liver cancer cells was five times that of chlorella." (Wu et al, 2005).

Earlier work at the University of California, Irvine showed that phycocyanin exhibited a positive effect in **removing plaque from the arteries** (Morcos et al, 1988). The authors stated that the properties that phycocyanin exhibited in their study "suggest potential therapeutic use for plaque localization and regression."

SOD: Superoxide Dismutase

The enzyme called "superoxide dismutase" or "SOD" was discovered in 1968. It has been called the "antioxidant catalyst." SOD was first used in an injectable form to treat **severe breathing problems, arthritis** and **cancer**. The human body can produce its own SOD; it is considered one of the fastest acting and most important antioxidants in protecting the body against harmful oxidative stress. The problem historically with SOD has been that, since it is an enzyme, it has been difficult to take SOD orally and obtain active absorption of this enzyme into the bloodstream and throughout the body. Enzymes are generally unstable and cannot withstand the harsh acids present in the human stomach; however, evidence suggests that Spirulina in tablet form does not thoroughly dissolve in the stomach. It is true that a portion of the Spirulina tablets are dissolved in the stomach, but also, a significant portion of the Spirulina tablets are dissolved in the intestines. Stomach acids are not present in the intestines so SOD can be absorbed in a stable, active state directly from the intestine into the bloodstream and then carried by the bloodstream throughout the body.

A great deal of research has been done on SOD. In a recent study done in Germany the researchers stated that "one of the most important antioxidant enzymes is superoxide dismutase which catalyzes the dismutation of superoxide radicals to hydrogen peroxide. The enzyme plays an important role…in theories of the mechanisms of **aging**." (Kowald et al, 2005) Another study done at the University of California, San Diego reported that SOD "protects cells from toxic, reactive oxygen species and may be involved in **age-related degeneration**." This study showed that the absence of SOD in mice resulted in **hearing loss** at an earlier age (Keithley et al, 2005) Another animal study done in Finland concluded that "compounds with SOD and catalase activities have shown promising results in animal models against a variety of oxidant exposures including **cigarette smoke in the lung**." (Kinnula 2005)

SOD is believed to have a great influence in **neurodegenerative diseases** in general. It is widely believed that oxidative stress plays a major role in neurodegenerative diseases, so effective antioxidants like SOD may play a preventive or corrective role in such diseases. "Evidence of oxidative stress is apparent in both acute and chronic neurodegenerative diseases, such as **stroke, Parkinson's disease and amyotrophic lateral sclerosis [ALS or "Lou Gehrig's disease]**. Increased generation of reactive oxygen species simply overwhelms endogenous antioxidant defenses, leading to subsequent oxidative damage and cell death…Antioxidant enzymes such as superoxide dismutase (SOD), catalase and glutathione peroxidase have demonstrated therapeutic efficacy in models of neurodegeneration." (Pong, 2003)

Another study done in Poland states that "the use of antioxidants as drugs that may control the inflammatory process recently has become widely studied...One of the most important components or antioxidant barriers in humans is superoxide dismutase. Experimental treatment with SOD proved to be effective in animals." (Renke et al, 2005) At the University of Colorado School of Medicine researchers pointed out that the space between individual cells is protected from oxidative stress by SOD, and that this activity is more highly pronounced in certain areas including **blood vessels, heart, lungs, kidney and in the placenta.** They pointed out that the loss of SOD activity "contributes to the pathogenesis of a number of diseases." (Nozik-Grayck et al, 2005)

Polysaccharides and "Calcium Spirulan"

Polysaccharides are another constituent of Spirulina that show promise of having great benefits in human nutrition. Calcium Spirulan is one such polysaccharide, which is separated out from a hot water extract of Spirulina. Japanese researchers have found excellent potential for Calcium Spirulan in different applications. In one experiment, Calcium Spirulan was found to inhibit the replication of several different viruses including **HIV-1, herpes simplex 1, measles, mumps, influenza, and human cytomegalovirus.** "It was found that Calcium Spirulan selectively inhibited the penetration of virus into host cells." (Hayashi et al, 1996) The same group of researchers from Toyama Medical and Pharmaceutical University performed another experiment in which Calcium Spirulan again showed excellent antiviral properties against HIV-1 and herpes simplex 1. The study said "Calcium Spirulan can be a candidate agent for an anti-HIV therapeutic drug that might overcome the disadvantages observed in many sulfated polysaccharides." (Hayashi et al, 1996)

A study done in 2001 at the University of Mississippi School of Pharmacy extracted a polysaccharide from Spirulina which they named "Immulina." They found that this polysaccharide has potent **immunostimulatory activity** in humans through activation of monocytes and macrophages, and that it also increases interleukin-1b and tumor necrosis factor alpha. They concluded that this polysaccharide is "between 100 and 1000 times more active for in vitro monocyte activation than polysaccharide preparations that are currently used for **cancer** immunotherapy." (Pugh et al, 2001)

24

Researchers in both Japan and China have examined the potential of Spirulina's polysaccharides in **cancer** therapy. In a study titled "Inhibition of tumor invasion and metastasis by Calcium Spirulan," scientists at Japan's Toyama Medical and Pharmaceutical University found that lung metastasis was significantly reduced by Calcium Spirulan by inhibiting tumor invasion of the cell membranes. A "marked decrease of **lung tumor** colonization" resulted (Mishima et al, 1998). The Chinese study was done on mice and dogs at the Medical and Pharmaceutical Academe of Yangzhou University. They found that the polysaccharides from Spirulina **increased the level of red blood cells, white blood cells, and hemoglobin in the blood**, and also increased nucleated cells in bone marrow of dogs. There conclusion: "Polysaccharide extract of Spirulina Platensis has **chemo-protective and radio-protective** capability, and may be a potential **adjunct to cancer therapy**." (Zhang et al, 2001)

Gamma Linolenic Acid (GLA)

In the quest for a healthier diet, we face a major adversary – dietary fat. We all know that fats and oils tend to be fattening – they help clog the arteries and expand the waistline. But good or unsaturated fatty acids are present in every cell and are essential for good health, performing many vital functions. Excess fats and oils cause harm by flooding our systems with the wrong kind of fatty acids, impeding the absorption of useful fatty acids.

Some useful fatty acids serve as building blocks for more complex biomolecules. Linoleic acid is classified as essential: the body needs it but cannot make it, so it must be supplied in the diet. Gamma linolenic acid (GLA) is synthesized from linoleic acid, and from GLA the body makes a very important hormone-like substance called prostaglandin E1 (PGE1). PGE1 helps to prevent **heart attacks and strokes, helps to remove excess fluid, improves circulation, slows down cholesterol production, improves nerve function, and regulates cell division** (Crisafi 1992). PGE1 is anti-inflammatory: it is vital to maintaining a healthy balance in our joints, helping to **prevent inflammation and pain**. Groups of **arthritis** sufferers have shown significant improvement after taking GLA supplements (Belch 1985; Kendler 1987). GLA has also been found to be an important nutrient for the prevention of certain skin disorders, such as **psoriasis** (Ziboh and Fletcher 1992); and it appears to alleviate **premenstrual syndrome** (PMS) (Horrobin 1983).

Evidence is mounting that factors such as stress, aging, alcohol consumption, and poor diet make it difficult for our bodies to convert linoleic acid to GLA. And some people simply have insufficient linoleic acid in their diets. This makes finding a dietary source of GLA very important. Fortunately, the plant world has a few good sources: Spirulina, black currant seed oil, oil of evening primrose, and borage seed oil are all rich in GLA. Of these, only Spirulina provides GLA in a whole food form, a form the body can efficiently use. In fact, Spirulina and mother's milk are the only natural food sources of GLA. The others are all extracted oil compounds. The concentration of GLA in Spirulina is remarkably high, so that five grams provide 50 milligrams while an evening primrose oil capsule of 500 milligrams provides 45 to 50 milligrams. And, unlike the other sources, Spirulina provides a wide range of additional nutrients.

Spirulina and mother's milk are the only natural foods to contain the fatty acid gamma linolenic acid (GLA). In testing both chlorella and Spirulina for GLA it was found that Spirulina had "unusually high levels of GLA, an essential polyunsaturated fatty acid." (Otles and Pire, 2001) GLA is being found useful in the treatment of **arthritis** (Belch et al 1988) and appears to be effective for other degenerative diseases (Kendler 1987) as well as **premenstrual syndrome** (Horrobin 1983).

A recent study about GLA's effect on **blood lipids** stated that "Essential fatty acids such as GLA can prevent accumulation of **cholesterol** in the body, and Spirulina has an appreciable amount of GLA...It can be concluded that Spirulina, rich in antioxidants, GLA, amino acids and fatty acids, helped reduce the increased levels of lipids in patients with hyperlipidemic nephrotic syndrome." (Samuels et al, 2002)

Vitamin B-12

Spirulina is an excellent source of Vitamin B-12. However, there is some unresolved controversy over exactly how much B-12 it contains. B-12 is essential for normal growth and neurological function; a deficiency causes **fatigue and moodiness**, and eventually **neurological damage**. The body does produce its own B-12 and can store it for years, but vegetarians in particular are susceptible to B-12 deficiency.

The richest sources of B-12 are meats – especially organ meats – and dairy foods. Spirulina, fermented foods such as miso, and certain sea vegetables were thought to contain high levels of B-12. However, research into the effects of these foods on B-12 levels in the body and on B-12 deficiency has shown that these foods may actually contain B-12 analogues that do not fulfill the biological requirements of the body. The Recommended Daily Allowance (RDA) of B-12 for adults is three micrograms. Using the government-approved microbiological assay, Spirulina was found to contain 2.2 micrograms of B-12 per gram. Thus, by taking 3 grams of Spirulina per day (in powder form or by taking six 500 mg tablets) you can get more than double the government approved RDA. To be fair, we must also consider the results of another testing method called a radioassay. With the radioassay method, a level of 0.4 micrograms of B-12 per gram was found. If we go by the lower radioassay figure, fifteen tablets or two-and-a-half teaspoons of Spirulina powder would provide the RDA. That still makes Spirulina a very good source of Vitamin B-12, containing more than a serving of fish or eggs.

Spirulina and Weight Loss

Losing weight is not easy, and Spirulina is helpful in more ways than one. Spirulina is extremely nutritious – high in complete protein, beta-carotene, B vitamins, minerals, gamma linolenic acid (GLA), enzymes, and micronutrients. Taking Spirulina before meals helps to satisfy the appetite so that one eats less at mealtimes and doesn't feel as hungry between meals.

Spirulina is a pure and natural whole food containing no synthetic ingredients or preservatives, and it is grown without pesticides or herbicides. Unlike diet pills, many of which require a prescription, Spirulina is totally safe with no dangerous side effects. Spirulina nourishes your body as it helps you to lose weight. It is non-addictive, and you do not develop a tolerance for it: In other words, you don't have to keep increasing the amount you take to achieve the same effect.

We feel hungry when blood glucose and amino acid reserves are low, so it is important to keep these levels high when dieting. The polysaccharides in Spirulina raise blood glucose levels, and all the essential amino acids are provided by Spirulina's complete, highly digestible protein. Spirulina does not have the hard cell wall characteristic of other plants, and so it is quickly and easily digested. Unlike meat and dairy protein, Spirulina is low-fat, low-calorie, and extremely low in cholesterol. The amino acid phenylalanine, which is found in Spirulina, is said to suppress the appetite by acting on the appetite center of the brain.

Low Energy

Since most people don't eat a well balanced diet to begin with, dieting can really put a strain on the body's nutrient supplies, making one feel tired and listless. Low-calorie diets that are also low in nutrients actually promote muscle loss and can prevent one from losing fat. Spirulina is such a concentrated food containing so many nutrients that it really helps to compensate for a shortage of other foods. The native people living near Lake Chad in Africa, an alkaline lake where Spirulina grows naturally, have been known to eat only Spirulina for months during times of famine, with no noticeable negative side effects. But we don't recommend that people do this, even if they're trying to lose weight. We recommend using Spirulina as an adjunct to any sensible diet plan.

Iron Deficiency

Iron deficiency is very common in women, who eat less food than men on average and lose iron during menstruation. Vegetarian women are especially prone to iron deficiency. While dieting, women often fail to eat large enough portions of iron-containing foods. Although the body only requires 1.5 mg of iron per day, the RDA (Recommended Dietary Allowance) for iron is 15 mg for women (30 mg for pregnant women). The assumption is that only ten percent of dietary iron is absorbed. The typical American diet contains six to seven mg of iron for every 1000 calories. Six tablets (three grams) of Hawaiian Spirulina contain 3.18 mg iron, the equivalent of 80 grams of liver or almost two cups of raw spinach. And the iron in Spirulina is easily absorbed by the body, making it more bioavailable.

Science of Nutrition

Nutrition is a new science, and we are still uncertain about which foods we should eat and in what combinations for maximum benefit. There are so many theories about diet and many of these are constantly being revised. The range of diets is bewildering, especially to those of us without a degree in nutrition. It can be argued that even professional nutritionists don't have the complete picture: Anyone who has eaten the average hospital diet with its white bread and Jell-O cannot be blamed for questioning its nutritional value.

Spirulina fits into practically any dietary plan because it is an extremely digestible, high-energy, low-calorie, low-fat natural food containing an incredibly wide range of important nutrients.

Crash Diets

Although health professionals warn of the dangers of crash diets, many people still use them. For someone who is a hundred pounds or so overweight, it can be disheartening to try to lose weight gradually, and so people take all sorts of drastic measures to lose as much weight as possible as quickly as possible – often with little thought for the body's nutritional needs. We highly recommend that people do not go on crash diets, but if they do they must realize the importance of taking food supplements. The concentrated nutrition of Spirulina can certainly help to counteract such an assault on the body by providing much of the nutrition that the body needs. Unfortunately, even when people lose weight on crash diets, they usually put the weight back on again rather quickly when they go off the diet. Losing and gaining weight constantly puts a strain on the system and is not recommended for good health.

Healthy and Safe Dieting

With Spirulina you can maintain high energy levels and know that you are getting the benefit of a super-nutritious food without consuming a lot of calories or fat: There are less than four calories in a gram of Spirulina. Take at least six tablets or a teaspoon of powder, which is roughly three grams, about an hour before meals. This helps to satisfy the appetite and reduce cravings. For some, taking Spirulina also reduces the desire for sweets and fried foods. You may want to experiment until you find the amount and the schedule that works best for you. If you tend to eat throughout the day, try taking a few tablets three times a day. If you eat more in the evenings, you may want to take all your Spirulina powder or tablets about an hour before dinner, or even after dinner.

Using Spirulina to help satisfy your appetite is a healthy and safe way to lose weight. Of course, we are not suggesting that you can eat junk food and make it all right by adding Spirulina. The rules of a healthy diet still apply: Eat lots of fresh fruits, vegetables, and whole grains; and cut down on fats, sugars, and processed foods. Eating smaller portions is obviously the key to losing weight, and this is where Spirulina helps. Eating slowly and chewing each mouthful thoroughly also helps.

Exercise

No health program is complete without exercise. Exercise keeps the heart strong, increases strength, helps us to release toxins, and is essential to lose fat and build muscle. It also speeds up the metabolism, making it easier to burn calories and lose weight. And of course, it makes us look and feel better, with more energy and stamina. It is important to try to find a type of exercise that you enjoy. What is easy and fun for one person is extremely difficult and dull for another. The more you enjoy exercising, the more likely you are to stick with it. It doesn't have to be conventional exercise either. Belly dancing or karate may be much more appealing to chronic non-exercisers than jogging or aerobics. And remember that Spirulina can give you the energy to make exercise more enjoyable.

The Ecology and Biology of Spirulina

Many of you will recall the scene from the motion picture Out of Africa where Robert Redford flies a plane over a lake covered with scattering flamingos. The lake was Lake Nakuru in Kenya, and the food the flamingos were eating was Spirulina. The rich flora of Lake Nakuru supports over a million flamingos, who sieve the algae with a specialized feather in their beaks. The flamingos even owe their famous pink plumage to pigments derived from the algae.

Pure and Simple Food

From the simplest elements – water, carbon dioxide, simple nitrogen and phosphorus, and sunlight – Spirulina creates an extremely concentrated and wonderfully complex food, rich in an astonishing array of nutrients. This is what is meant by being low on the food chain.

Harvesting the Sun's Energy

The driving force behind this synthesis is the intense power of the sun. Spirulina fathers light with an organization of remarkable pigments, including the blue and green compounds, which give it the classification of blue-green algae. The green in blue-green algae is chlorophyll. The blue is phycocyanin which is found only in blue green algae species. The presence of phycocyanin in Spirulina helps account for its extremely high concentration of vegetarian protein.

Harvesting sunlight creates a problem for Spirulina. Spirulina needs as much sunlight as possible but must be protected from burning, especially in a shallow cultivation pond. Imagine lying out in the hot tropical sun all day long, 365 days a year. You would certainly go through a lot of sunscreen! To protect itself, Spirulina produces carotenoids, "Nature's Sunscreen." The hotter the sun, the more sunscreen is needed, and the more carotenoids are produced. Tropical areas are thus better suited to Spirulina production than temperate areas. Spirulina farms in non-tropical regions must shut down for 3 or 4 months a year due to insufficient amount of sunshine. But on the other hand, Spirulina farms in areas that get very hot may also have to shut down during the hot season because the heat and sunlight may kill the algae. To our knowledge, Spirulina grown at Cyanotech's farm in Hawaii is the only Spirulina in the world that successfully grows twelve months per year. This continuous cultivation for over 20 years has allowed Hawaiian Spirulina to become the most carotenoid-rich Spirulina in the world (by far).

Spirulina — Cultured and Clean

Cultured Versus Wild

Many have asked the question, which is better, cultured Spirulina or wild blue-green algae collected from lakes? First, we suggest that the health-minded consumer try the products. How do the various products taste – clean or bitter? How does one feel after eating them? Is the product reasonably priced?

Cultured algae have several major advantages. One way to view this is to consider the history of corn. At first it grew wild, and fossil evidence indicates that the original corn ears were tiny, the size of a finger. Generations of Native Americans developed and bred new strains: Their skills and techniques led to the development of the modern staple varieties, which are hardier, larger, and more nutritious than their wild forerunners.

The development of Spirulina has taken a similar path, but because a generation of corn takes a whole year to grow, and Spirulina takes less than a week, the process has been much faster. Selecting from literally millions of billions of cells, aquaculturists have succeeded in developing superior strains of microalgae.

Growers in Hawaii add nutrients from one of the deepest, cleanest oceans on the planet. Clean, pure deep ocean water is pumped from 2000 feet (approximately 600 meters) below the surface of the ocean and added to Hawaiian Spirulina. This deep ocean water is rich in trace minerals and elements. Scientists estimate that this deep ocean water hasn't been to the surface for over 2000 years—this is indeed very special water. Hawaiian Spirulina has been developed into a uniquely nutritious and potent species of Spirulina that has several times the carotenoid levels of wild strains of blue-green algae along with 94 minerals and trace elements.

Quality and Purity

Another very important reason for growing cultured microalgae is to control purity. Cultivated Spirulina ponds are sampled every day and carefully examined for any sign of contamination, ensuring that the consumer receives a pure product. Scientists believe there are over 30,000 species of microalgae. The immense range of species includes nutritious varieties like Spirulina and chlorella, as well as potentially dangerous species such as the microcystis strains identified in Klamath Lake, Oregon, where a commercially sold blue green algae product is harvested. Microcystis is an alga that is toxic to the human liver. One must think of microalgae like mushrooms—common cultured table mushrooms are absolutely safe and healthful while others, such as some toadstools, can be poisonous. While microcystis has appeared in wild harvested blue green microalgae products in the past, it has never been found in cultured Spirulina.

The microalgae farmer's "field" is a pond and the "seed" is a live culture. Ponds are lined with food-quality liners covered with a layer of natural calcium carbonate (which coral is composed of). Paddlewheels gently stir the cultures, ensuring optimum light for each cell and helping the pond to release oxygen. The culture thrives in these ideal conditions, growing several times faster than it would in the wild.

High Productivity

Cultured Spirulina grows extremely fast: In fact, Spirulina farms are the most productive agricultural systems in the world. A typical output for year-round production, such as that realized in Hawaii, is over 400,000 kilograms a year on just 45 hectares of land. When you consider that Spirulina is typically 60% protein, that means over 240,000 kilograms of pure protein is produced each year, far surpassing the per-hectare yields of high-protein crops such as soybeans and triticale wheat. And, unlike other forms of farming, there is no fertilizer or manure runoff to pollute ground water or streams. It's refreshing to know that the world's most productive agricultural systems are non-polluting and use no herbicides or pesticides!

Harvesting

Spirulina is a filamentous algae (meaning that it grows in strands), a shape that allows for harvesting by stainless steel screens. This method uses far less energy than centrifugation (which is used for chlorella, another microalgae) and is gentle on the cells. While the Spirulina is being sieved out on screens, it is given several fresh water washes, ensuring a clean product with a fresh taste.

Ponds are harvested to 70% of their depth, with what remains being the seed for the next generation. It's like mowing the lawn – the part left behind grows again.

Drying Methods

After washing, the harvested paste is then fed into a dryer. A great deal of research has gone into methods of protecting the nutrient quality during the drying process. Because freeze-drying minimizes exposure to heat, it was an early choice in the effort to produce a high-quality product. The other advantage of freeze-drying is that the particles produced disperse rapidly in water, thus making a convenient drink ingredient. The downside of freeze-drying is that the wet product is exposed to oxygen for many hours while it freezes. Usually the frozen blocks then sit on dryer pans in freezer trucks while they travel to freeze drying companies. Many people don't realize that the freeze-drying process also involves the use of heat during the later stages, after much of the moisture content has been drawn off. Thus, freeze-drying is not the drying method of choice for Spirulina because this process can lead to losses of vital nutrients—carotenoids, antioxidants and enzymes.

Spray dryers have traditionally been used for Spirulina. One benefit of spray drying is the extremely short duration of time that the product is exposed to oxygen. Within minutes of harvest, the product is dried. It travels through the dryer for a few seconds and is then quickly packaged. The primary disadvantage of spray drying is the use of heat. Although it is of short duration, the temperature is elevated and enzyme damage is a concern. Spirulina producers have taken this into consideration and run their dryers at low temperatures. The product is always kept well below boiling, minimizing damage.

Ocean-Chill™ Drying

The most significant advancement in drying has been the development of Ocean-Chill Drying (U.S. Patent #5,276,977). Scientists in Hawaii have developed a closed-cycle modified spray drying system which uses very cold sea water from 600 meters below the surface of the ocean to remove moisture and chill the air in the dryer. This chilling and dehumidifying allows for the elimination of oxygen from the dryer, effecting a significant increase in the retention of carotenoid and enzyme activity. With Ocean-Chill Drying, the Spirulina dries in

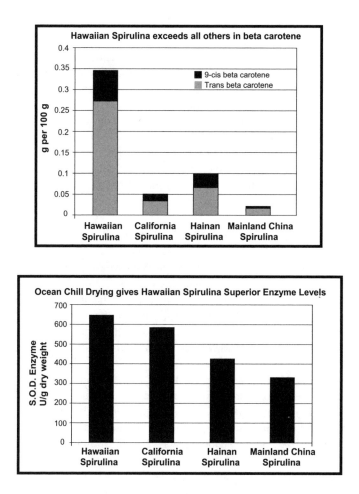

Hawaiian Spirulina exceeds all others in beta carotene

g per 100 g

- ■ 9-cis beta carotene
- ▨ Trans beta carotene

Hawaiian Spirulina | California Spirulina | Hainan Spirulina | Mainland China Spirulina

Ocean Chill Drying gives Hawaiian Spirulina Superior Enzyme Levels

S.O.D. Enzyme U/g dry weight

Hawaiian Spirulina | California Spirulina | Hainan Spirulina | Mainland China Spirulina

about three seconds and with less than 1% oxygen present. Data from independent laboratories show that Spirulina dried by this method contains substantially higher levels of carotenoids and enzymes than Spirulina dried by any other method, including freeze-drying.

Tabletting

Tablet preparation is another area requiring careful attention to quality. Tablets are essentially a powder mixture squeezed into a mold. In general, to manufacture tablets at high speed, the tabletter must either add a large amount of binder or excipient to the powder or granulate the powder prior to tabletting, exposing the product to oxidation. Granulation is a process of wetting the product and then heating it for hours in trays.

An alternative, more expensive method is to formulate tablets with vastly reduced excipient and run the tablet presses slowly. This produces a better tasting tablet and eliminates the need for granulation. The tablets come off the press warm but never hot, reducing the chance of nutritional loss. High-quality tablets from Spirulina farms in Hawaii and California are manufactured in this way.

Sources of Spirulina

It is important to know the source from which your Spirulina comes. There are vast differences in the technology and production techniques of different Spirulina farms. For example, many commercial farms have very poor hygiene during their production which leads to high bacterial counts. In many cases these farms irradiate their Spirulina to bring the bacterial counts down, but this has the adverse effect of lowering enzyme, carotenoid, and antioxidant levels.

Another extremely important factor is the environment in which the Spirulina is grown. Algae are very absorptive; they soak up impurities in the air and water as they grow. Thus, the cleanliness and purity of the water and air are essential to have a quality finished product. Spirulina farms in Asia are notorious for having high lead and heavy metal traces in their Spirulina, because many of these farms are located in areas with air pollution or impure water sources. The founders of Cyanotech Corporation chose the Kona coast of Hawaii as the perfect place to grow Spirulina over twenty years ago not only because of the abundant sunshine, but also because of the purity of the air and water. Kona is on the Big Island of Hawaii, three islands away from the hustle and bustle of Hawaii's capital city of Honolulu. The clean air on this remote island is ideal for growing high quality Spirulina. And Cyanotech uses water from two different sources—deep sea water from 600 meters below the ocean's surface and municipal drinking water from the Hawaiian aquifer. Cyanotech pays for its water while (to our knowledge) every other Spirulina farm in the world uses river or irrigation water to grow their Spirulina. You can't help but have a purer product when you start with purer water.

Only USA-Grown Spirulina Safe as Food

A very significant development in the world of Spirulina took place in 2004 when the United States government accepted a petition made by Cyanotech Corporation and Earthrise Farms (grown in California) to have their Spirulina recognized as safe for use in all food, beverage and supplement prooducts. These two farms are currently the only two in the world that have qualified for this status, demonstrating their high quality and purity. If you purchase Spirulina grown outside the United States, you can never be sure of its quality.

Organic versus All Natural Hawaiian Spirulina

Another critical development took place just before the second edition of this book was published. In October 2002 the US National Organic Standards Board (NOSB) voted to continue to allow the use of mined Chilean nitrate in Spirulina production until October 2005. (Chilean nitrate is an all natural, water soluble form of nitrogen used in the production of Organic Spirulina.) Unfortunately, the USDA organic production regulations are directed at terrestrial farming and do not address the unique position occupied by aquatic farming of crops such as Spirulina. Production of Spirulina requires water soluble forms of phosphorus and nitrogen. This is not desired in terrestrial farming as soluble forms of phosphorous and nitrogen can harm the soil and contaminate ground water. On the other hand, this is not a problem in Spirulina production because all culture ponds are lined and there is no runoff or contamination of ground water. The NOSB voted to disallow the use of Chilean nitrate in October 2005 as it can lead to contamination of ground water and is mined and thus not considered a sustainable source of nitrogen.

With Chilean nitrate prohibited in all organic production systems, an alternative source of organic soluble nitrogen must be found. The only sources of soluble nitrogen allowed under organic regulations are compost teas of animal and plant waste material and various manures. The scientists at Cyanotech have examined these potential sources of soluble nitrogen and found them unsatisfactory because they would:

1) Contaminate Spirulina with lead and other heavy metals
2) Increase the bacterial count in Spirulina
3) Produce inferior Spirulina products at a much higher cost

For these reasons, Cyanotech stopped production of organic Spirulina in October, 2005. Instead, Cyanotech is concentrating its efforts on continually improving the quality of All Natural Hawaiian Spirulina Pacifica products.

In many ways standard Spirulina culture methods (not organic) are compatible with traditional organic growing systems. Spirulina does not create any ground water pollution or soil erosion since it is grown in lined ponds. Water and energy are used much more efficiently than in terrestrial agriculture use (including organic systems). Cyanotech's All Natural Spirulina products are GMO free, are produced without the use of pesticides or herbicides, are produced using pure Hawaiian aquifer water and deep seawater as a source of trace minerals and use the patented Ocean Chill™ drying process to preserve oxygen sensitive nutrients. Hawaiian Spirulina from Cyanotech has the highest purity, and by far the highest nutritional value of any Spirulina available.

Cyanotech has heard that some foreign producers are going to continue to produce "organic Spirulina," and our scientists do not believe that this can be done in an honest way and maintain any level of quality. For example, the non-organic Spirulina of one of these producers was tested at an independent laboratory. This laboratory's test results showed that the Spirulina from this producer had very high levels of lead and other heavy metals as well as other quality concerns. Please remember that this was a non-organic product; when this farm switches to compost teas or animal manures as they claim to be doing to produce an organic product, Cyanotech's scientists believe that their heavy metal and bacterial levels will be off the charts.

Cyanotech and Earthrise Farms of California have been producing Spirulina the longest of any farms, and Cyanotech was the first to obtain organic certification, and Earthrise the second, under the old standard that allowed Chilean nitrate. These two leading farms have the greatest scientists and Spirulina production know-how of any producers in the world, and yet after over three years of research both Cyanotech and Earthrise decided that high quality Spirulina could not be produced under the new standard.

Comparison -	All Natural U.S. Grown Spirulina	"Organic" Spirulina Produced Under the New Standard
Pesticide Free	✔	✔
Herbicide Free	✔	✔
Environmentally Friendly	✔	✔
Purified Nutrients	✔	
Low Bacterial Count	✔	
Low Heavy Metal Level	✔	
Non-Animal Fertilizers	✔	
Minimally Processed	✔	
Higher Growth Rate	✔	

Supporting the Environment

There is a popular myth about Spirulina helping to reverse the greenhouse effect by removing carbon dioxide from the atmosphere and producing abundant oxygen. Spirulina does remove and store carbon dioxide and does produce oxygen. Unfortunately, the carbon dioxide is released when we eat and digest the algae. We breathe in oxygen to digest the algae and then breathe out the carbon dioxide (which was incorporated in the algae), and it returns to the atmosphere.

Spirulina may not be able to save our planet, but we can. As consumers, we are faced with choices that affect the environment every day. Choosing pesticide and herbicide-free food is one way of ensuring that these harmful chemcals do not enter the environment or our bodies. We can also carefully select foods and other products on the basis of packaging, eschewing the excessive use of plastic and other hard-to-recycle materials.

Glass has significant environmental benefits over plastic. First, the raw materials of glass are primarily sand and limestone, whereas the raw materials of plastic are petrochemicals. Petrochemicals originate in oil-producing areas such as Iraq and Alaska – two areas that have been devastated as a consequence of oil. The production of plastics involves the use of solvent chemistry, which results in considerably more air pollution than that created by glass production. Finally, plastic is difficult to recycle. Many areas still do not offer recycling of plastic,

39

and those that do struggle with the many different types and the difficulty of shipping such bulky materials. Glass is being readily accepted as a recycled material all over the nation – it is recycled at about ten times the rate of plastic. Also, glass is an excellent barrier to oxygen and moisture and imparts no residues to the product.

Recycling glass means using up fewer natural resources, reducing air and water pollution, and saving energy in the manufacturing process.

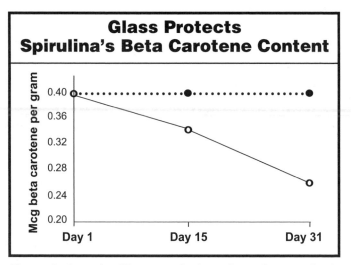

Glass Protects Spirulina's Beta Carotene Content

The graph shows the difference packaging makes – the upper line is Spirulina in glass, the lower line is in plastic. The Spirulina in the plastic container lost 38% of its beta-carotene in the first month while that in the glass container lost none.

Glass Versus Plastic Packaging

Oxygen is a very small molecule – small enough to go right through plastic and destroy the antioxidants present in Spirulina. For example, the natural beta-carotene in Spirulina, unlike synthetic, is not stabilized with preservatives, and it must be protected from oxygen.

Spirulina should be stored in oxygen-resistant packaging. Once the package has been opened, it should be kept in the refrigerator if possible. The best packaging for Spirulina should have a metal cap with a rubber seal and an

40

oxygen absorber with a glass bottle.

Water and Land Use

Water and land use are two important environmental factors that we must consider. The figures presented below show the differences between eating low and high on the food chain.

Spirulina can thrive in many places where no other crop will survive because it requires no soil and relatively little water. Hawaiian Spirulina, for example, is grown on a barren coastal lava flow.

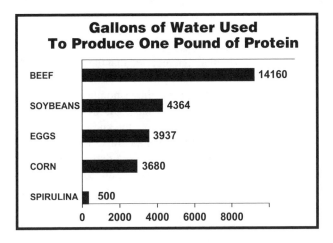

Gallons of Water Used To Produce One Pound of Protein

BEEF	14160
SOYBEANS	4364
EGGS	3937
CORN	3680
SPIRULINA	500

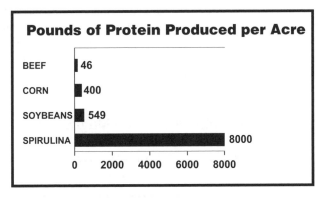

Pounds of Protein Produced per Acre

BEEF	46
CORN	400
SOYBEANS	549
SPIRULINA	8000

Spirulina's History as a Food

The Aztecs

Spirulina needs to grow in very alkaline water; it grew wild in the great soda lakes of Central Mexico where it was prized by the Aztecs. Bernal Diaz del Castillo, who traveled to Mexico with the conqueror Cortés in 1519, wrote about the vast and crowded city marketplace, where everything from precious jewels and medicines to animals and pottery made a dazzling display. A more unusual commodity, but one highly prized throughout Mexico, was tecuitlatl, or small cakes of Spirulina, which the Aztecs traded in the same way the Europeans traded cheese. Cortés and the Spanish were puzzled by this "blue-green mud." They never acquired a taste for tecuitlatl, but reported that the Aztecs found it delicious. The Aztecs collected Spirulina from the surface of the lakes with fine meshed nets and filled their canoes with it. On shore, they smoothed the earth into flat beds and spread the Spirulina out to dry in the sun. The wet paste, which was about three to four centimeters thick, would dry to a thickness of two to three millimeters. Various translations of the conquistadors' travel journals have led to some confusion about how the Indians actually ate tecuitlatl. Apparently, it was made into a bread, which tasted something like cheese, mixed with some grain dishes, and put into a sauce called chilmolli, which was made from tomatoes, chili peppers, and various spices.

It is said that the emperor Montezuma loved to eat fish. Unfortunately, the closest fresh fish was in the Gulf of Mexico, which was about 180 miles from the emperor's palace. So, it fell to the marathon runners to provide him with the catch of the day. These athletes were known to run up to a hundred miles a day, and Spirulina was an essential part of their diet. Stopping for a brief rest, they would take some Spirulina from the pouches they carried and mix up a batch with water to give them energy and endurance.

The Toltecs and the Mayas

It is quite probable that the Toltecs, who were overrun by the Aztecs, also relied on Spirulina as a source of nutrition. The Aztecs adopted many aspects of the Toltec and Mayan cultures.

There is evidence that the Mayas of Central America, whose civilization was at its height from about 300 to 900 A.D., cultivated Spirulina in the network of waterways that was also used for irrigating crops.

Kanembu of Lake Chad

Spirulina has been eaten for centuries by the Kanembu people, who live along the shores of Lake Chad in north-central Africa. It remains one of their main sources of protein.

The Spirulina is pushed to shore by the wind, where it concentrates into thick mats. The Kanembu women wade into the water trailing finely woven baskets behind them. They skim the surface to collect the algae, and the excess water flows out of the basket. The sludge is then transferred to clay pots or gourds. In the dunes bordering the lakes, the women dig holes in the warm sand in which they place shallow layers of the harvested paste. As the water drains into the sand and the Spirulina begins to dry, they mark it off into squares. The tropical sun soon transforms the paste into a dry biscuit, which is known as dihé.

Millet, which is the basis of almost every meal, is served with various spicy sauces, usually containing dihé, tomatoes, chili peppers, and spices. Beans, onions, and fish or meat are added if they are available. Dihé is an important ingredient of the sauce, eaten in about seven out of ten meals, and ten to twelve grams per person is used. Dihé is eaten plain by pregnant women, who believe that its color will protect their unborn babies from the eyes of sorcerers.

NASA

Spirulina's recent history includes being considered by NASA as a food to be taken into space. Spirulina would be an ideal food to grow in a closed system such as a space station because it grows very quickly, takes up very little space, and its nutrient requirements could be met by recycled waste, in exchange for which it would provide the inhabitants with oxygen and concentrated nutrition.

Feeding the Hungry

Spirulina is an ideal food for malnourished populations; and self-sus-

43

taining farms are being set up in some Third World villages and other communities where arable land is scarce and crop harvests are unpredictable.

Dr. Ripley Fox, a pioneering microbiologist, devotes himself to studying and implementing ways to end malnutrition, especially in Third World villages. Food handouts don't solve the problem: Insufficient quantities, corruption, spoilage, and lack of good roads and transportation all contribute to their inadequacy. Dr. Fox says that no industrial production of food can help these rural poor. Without money, they cannot participate with industry. They must feed themselves, and we can help them by introducing new food technologies appropriate to the village situation (Fox 1985). Dr. Fox helped set up Integrated Village Health and Energy Systems – low-cost systems which enable villagers to grow their own Spirulina using recycled village waste and solar technology. The criticism that people will not change their food habits to include Spirulina in their diets has proved invalid. After setting up demonstration projects in India, Togo, Senegal, and Peru, Dr. Fox and his team are now ready to guide others in developing village Spirulina farms.

At the Togo project, babies suffering from severe malnutrition were fed ten to fifteen grams of Spirulina a day dissolved in gruel. After three months, the babies were up to normal weight and activity (Fox 1987).

Spirulina Recipes

Spirulina can be taken in tablet or powder form. For those who prefer the powder, there are a growing number of recipes available, some of which disguise the taste, and some of which enhance it. Many users simply mix their Spirulina with water, but that is certainly not for everyone. Spirulina does not dissolve in liquids, but becomes suspended, so it must be vigorously shaken or made into a paste with a small amount of liquid before being added to soups or stews.

Once you get used to the color – and it is an intense color – you can enjoy Spirulina in many everyday dishes. Mixed in chili, for example, you can barely taste the Spirulina, but the chili does turn a rather strange color You can go to town on St. Patrick's Day by adding Spirulina to fruit punch, beer, cake icing, and ice cream. Any time you need a natural green food coloring, Spirulina is the perfect choice. Remember, it is extremely concentrated, so very little is needed.

44

Although Spirulina cookies and breads are delicious, it really is a pity to cook Spirulina because prolonged heat destroys much of the nutrient content. When adding it to soups or stews, it is best to do so just before serving. Spirulina can be added to almost any salad dressing or sprinkled over a salad.

Here are some simple recipes you may like to try:

Spirulina with Fruit Juice

Begin with a teaspoonful of Spirulina mixed with fruit juice in a blender or with an electric mixer. Apple, pineapple, or papaya work the best. You can increase the amount of Spirulina to suit your taste and your personal health program.

Spirulina Smoothie

2 bananas
Half cup yogurt, one cup soymilk, or one cup of fruit juice (apple, orange, or pineapple)
One or more of the following:
1 papaya, 1 peach, 1 mango, half cup of boysenberries or raspberries
1 teaspoon Spirulina
Blend all ingredients

Papaya Spirulina Smoothie

1 ripe papaya   ¼ teaspoon cinnamon
1 teaspoon Spirulina   Juice of one lime
Blend all ingredients

Spirulina Salsa

Add one teaspoon of Spirulina to a bowl of salsa. The Spirulina enhances the taste and gives the salsa an interesting color and a nice texture.

Guacamole

2 avocados   Cayenne pepper
2 medium tomatoes   Fresh lime juice to taste
2 tablespoons salsa   Salt to taste
1 teaspoon Spirulina   1 tablespoon finely chopped onion

Mash avocados. Add all other ingredients and blend well. Spirulina gives guacamole a beautiful color.

Avocado Dip
1 avocado
1 tablespoon sour cream
1 teaspoon Spirulina
Mash all ingredients together

Paprika to taste
Tamari or soy sauce to taste

Cream Dip
4 tablespoons sour cream or non-fat yogurt
Juice of one lemon
3 teaspoons tamari or soy sauce
1 teaspoon Spirulina
Mix all ingredients together

Another Cream Dip
4 tablespoons sour cream or non-fat yogurt
½ teaspoon garam masala & ¼ teaspoon cumin, or ¾ teaspoon curry powder
3 teaspoons tamari or soy sauce
1 teaspoon Spirulina
Small clove garlic
Mix all ingredients together

Tofu Salad
8 ounces firm tofu
2 medium tomatoes
1 medium grated carrot
2 spring onions, finely chopped

1 bell pepper (green or red)
1 medium zucchini
2 stalks celery
1 tablespoon tamari or soy sauce

Generous pinch of basil, thyme, and marjoram
Hot pepper sauce or cayenne pepper (to taste)
1 heaped teaspoon Spirulina
Mix all ingredients together. Almost any combination of raw vegetables can be put into a tofu salad.

Pesto (pasta sauce)
1 packed cup fresh basil leaves
2 tablespoons parmesan cheese
2 teaspoons Spirulina

3-5 tablespoons virgin olive oil
3 cloves garlic
Pinch of salt

2 ounces pine nuts, macadamia nuts, almonds, or walnuts
Blend all ingredients

Rice Topping

3 tablespoons soy sauce
Dried bonito (optional)

1 tablespoon roasted sesame seeds
1 teaspoon Spirulina

Combine all ingredients and serve over rice

Spirulina Paté

Juice of half lemon
1 tablespoon olive oil
1 teaspoon Spirulina

1 teaspoon soy sauce
1 clove crushed garlic

Mix the Spirulina with the garlic. Add the lemon juice and soy sauce, and mix well with a fork. Stir in the olive oil. Serve on toast or crackers with slices of tomato and onion (optional).

Popcorn

Grated parmesan cheese
½ tablespoon dulse flakes
(or other seaweed)

Garlic powder (to taste)
Cayenne pepper, chili pepper, or paprika
1 tablespoon Spirulina

Make popcorn as usual. Mix together any or all of the above ingredients. While popcorn is still warm, add seasoning mixture and shake vigorously so that popcorn is evenly coated.

Enjoy!

Testimonials

Testimonials from the United States

Publisher's Note: The testimonials in this book are not intended to imply that Spirulina can cure or prevent any disease, nor are they intended as an aid in diagnosing or treating any disease.

People taking Spirulina report finding relief from arthritis and other painful conditions, seeing improvement in skin conditions, feeling more energetic, losing weight, and generally experiencing an increased sense of well-being. Here are some excerpts from letters that were sent to the offices of Cyanotech in Hawaii. While these are not scientific studies, they do show how people feel a difference in their health when using Spirulina from Cyanotech.

Arthritic Condition: Reiter's Syndrome

I just wanted to let you know how Spirulina changed my life. Two and a half years ago, when I was 29, I developed a painful arthritic condition known as Reiter's Syndrome. [My doctor gave me a prescription drug] which only upset my stomach and gave me vertigo. By this time, I was finding it difficult to sleep, let alone walk, and I was forced to quit my job. [Then my doctor gave me another prescription drug] which brought me some relief during the acute stage. The main drawback, besides its exorbitant price, was that it was very hard on my stomach. I spent the next six months in a state of nausea. I was able to walk short distances but it still hurt like hell.

Then one day a friend gave me some Spirulina; after a few days something wonderful happened – I realized I had no pain. I didn't attribute it to the Spirulina, however – I thought it was a natural occurrence. After a few weeks, I ran out of Spirulina, and sure enough, those nagging aches began to return. After a few painful days, I finally hit myself on the head and said, "It was the Spirulina!"

Since that day, about 6 months ago, I've never been without Spirulina. Not only has my arthritis disappeared, my overall mental and physical state is better. Thanks to Spirulina, I wake up each morning feeling fine and able to do things I was afraid I would never be able to do again. What can I say? Spirulina is the greatest! *(M. Simon, Fullerton, CA)*

48

Chronic Fatigue Syndrome

These wonderful tablets gave me back my strength. I suffered from Chronic Fatigue Syndrome...I will never quit taking your tablets. *(H. Nowak, Helen, GA)*

Energy/Resistance to Illness

I seem to be more energetic. I have better resistance to illness—it boosts my immune system. *(Carlene Kreetlove, Mazomani, WI)*

Eyesight/Skin/Menstrual Pains

Spirulina in tablets and powder has helped me and my family a lot. My eyesight has recovered from blurred vision. I have very tight sleep. Most of my pimples are gone and my face became more beautiful, not only because of smooth skin, but my eyes sparkle and dark spots around my eyes are gone. My menstruation pains are totally gone also. I feel really better. Thanks to Spirulina and God for such a wonderful discovery. *(Ellen Dimabayao, Los Angeles, CA)*

Body Pains

This is an excellent product which has put the desire to live back in me. Before I started the tablets I was so miserable with pain of all kinds all over my body, shooting pains, tired pain in my hip, aches in my calves.

I am now improved so that I can exercise, which is also good for me. My diet has not changed much nor my medication for diabetes and hypertension. However, my feeling is vastly different. I have told many others and started my two sisters and a fellow worker on it. I hope they are helped by it too, although mine was an extreme case which medical doctors and chiropractors couldn't seem to help. *(M. Honmyo, Seattle, WA)*

Energy/Appetite Suppressant/Mental & Cognitive Improvement

I am a Nutritional Health Advisor, Chef, Yoga Practitioner and Teacher,

Drummer and Writer. In over ten years of veganism I have tried many brands of Spirulina and Nutrex [Hawaiian] is by far the freshest and most potent form available on the market today. This has been confirmed by many nutritionist and scientist colleagues of mine. As a raw and living foodist, I consume Spirulina almost every day and it is one of my main sources of protein. I will never forget the first time I tried Nutrex Hawaiian Spirulina; I had boundless energy, my appetite decreased and I finally felt like my brain was functioning adequately. This product has increased my mental and cognitive capacities remarkably! If you want to understand what is meant by the statement "we use less than 2% of our brain," try this product and you will feel yourself accessing the remaining 98%. *(Shanti Devi Michal, New York City)*

Dark Spots on Face

A couple of months before I started taking Spirulina, my doctor warned me to watch a couple of dark spots on my face. These spots were presumably caused by sun exposure damaging my skin. After my wife saw Spirulina recommended by a news letter, we both added it to our diet. To my delight the spots on my face got smaller and disappeared after just a few months. *(Emil Eastburn, Westford, MA)*

Leg Pain

I am seventy years of age. At the time [I started taking Spirulina tablets] I was having severe pain in my knees and legs, which became much worse when I would lay down. I couldn't kneel and had difficulty even bending my knees. Now I am able to bend my knees and even do knee bends. I am very happy to say I no longer have the pains in my knees.

I am so happy to have discovered these miracle tablets. I feel so much better, not only with my knees and legs, but also in my general health. *(N. Behling, Palm Bay, FL)*

Internal Hemorrhoids

My husband has internal hemorrhoids and Spirulina has controlled them remarkably. *(Paula Cramer, Salt Lake City, UT)*

Energy/Mental Acuity/Immune System

I have a higher level of energy and mental acuity. It appears to strengthen my immune system. *(Pete Bauer, Mazomani, WI)*

Neck Pain

Several years ago, I took [a prescription drug] for severe neck pain. I stopped taking it when my sister told me about Spirulina. I seldom have any discomfort in this area now. [The prescription drug] was not nearly as effective as Spirulina. *(N. Hawkins, Indio, CA)*

Pre-Menstrual Syndrome/Appetite Suppressant

Nutrex Spirulina [Hawaiian] has been like a miracle cure for the severe PMS symptoms I suffered with for years. It's helped to ease tension and insomnia. Also it has acted as an appetite suppressant. I am very grateful. Thanks. *(Victoria Yiannatsis, Rehoboth Beach, DE)*

Arthritis/Energy

I am a 63 year old woman, have always been very active, and still have a cleaning service where I do a lot of the work myself. I've known for several years that I have the telltale signs of arthritis, the swollen joints in my fingers and a very tender lump on one of my knuckles. I was beginning to think I would have to give up my business as I was in so much pain, especially in my hands. Also, my ankles made a cracking noise when I walked.

A friend of mine told me about Spirulina and I thought, well I might as well give it a try. After taking Spirulina for three weeks, the first thing I noticed was that all the soreness and pain were gone from my hands and that my ankles didn't make a noise when I walked. After my second bottle, I could work eight and ten hours straight and still no pain.

I was out of Spirulina after my third bottle and after two weeks the soreness and pain had returned. After starting back on Spirulina, within four days all the swelling and pain are gone. I have more energy and just feel better all over. I've stopped taking all my other vitamins. I find that taking three tablets in the morning and three at bedtime works best for me.

I've recommended Spirulina to several of my friends and family members who are now taking it with positive results. I know for myself I don't want to be without Spirulina again. *(A. Walls, Melbourne, FL)*

Strength/Energy

I wish to tell you how much I appreciate the introduction to your Spirulina. I first became aware of the product when I asked a neighbor what her secret was in keeping in such good shape and how she gets so much energy. She told me that she had eaten your Spirulina for one year, and gets the energy from this product.

I was at that time in the process of moving, and was afraid, by doing all the work myself, I would hurt myself again, especially my shoulders (bursitis), and back (old age, I guess). I am 59 years old.

I started to eat 6 Spirulina tablets daily, two weeks before moving. Needless to say, I got through all with flying colors, experienced strength I had not known for a long time.

Thank you for making this product available to me. I feel younger, better, stronger, can work better with more energy. I am recommending your Spirulina to my friends, and for a good deed, I get them started with a first supply. *(E. Corderoy, Hilo, HI)*

Resistance to Colds/Energy/Pain

I have been taking Spirulina for six months. Mostly six tablets a day, sometimes more. I started taking your Spirulina when I had a painful condition in my right knee from what I thought was arthritis. Within two weeks, I had no pain left. It also gave me so much energy. I have not been hungry between meals.

I also noticed that I do not get colds and that during the flu season, even though I was in contact with my family who did have the flu, I did not get it. I know that when I forget to take Spirulina my symptoms returned. I know this natural product is from God. I recommend it to anyone. Thank you. *(C.B. Lang, Indiatlantic, FL)*

Arthritis

I am 64 years of age and have had a bone density test. They determined I have arthritis in two vertebrae, pelvic bone, and knee joint. I was in so much pain it was hard to walk any distance and had trouble sleeping, as I would wake with severe pain in my entire right leg.

When I first heard about Spirulina I did not think it would work but I was willing to give it a try. After three weeks, I can now walk two miles without pain. I thank God for Spirulina and for Clara who told me about it. *(L. Enmon, Ontario, Canada)*

Stamina/Energy

I feel better in the mornings and have more stamina and energy. *(D. Waki, Wailuku, HI)*

Cancer/Macular Degeneration/Pain

When I was 65, I had a routine physical exam and blood test at the VA Hospital in Honolulu. A few days later the doctor called me and said something seemed wrong with my blood. He was sending the sample to the military hospital (the Tripler Army Hospital and Medical Center). I became scared. After that the doctors sent me for more tests at the oncology department blood lab. They took ten blood samples during three days of tests, including bone scans. These tests were sent for analysis and profiles on the blood plasma cells. They found too many antibodies and too much protein in the blood. The tests, the doctors said, meant that I had multiple myeloma. He said to me, "I've got bad news, this is cancer of the blood and there is no cure for it. You will be dead in four months."

I not only felt rotten by this time because of the diagnosis, I just felt rotten in my body. I looked like a scarecrow. I had lost lots of weight. I often felt like keeling over when I was standing. I had no energy. During this time I had to go to Honolulu every month for analysis and treatment. I did that for about a year.

The doctor had not started me on chemotherapy in the first few months. I had heard of wheatgrass and the effects its high content of chlorophyll had on the blood. I had started taking wheat grass juice very early after my diagnosis. I drank at least two, eight ounce glasses a day for almost a year. I even grew the wheatgrass myself.

Tests showed that my health condition sort of maintained itself during the wheatgrass time, but I still felt rotten. I prayed every day. My tests involved bone lesions, nuclear isotope bone scans, and all during the later six months he kept testing my blood, weight, and more blood tests. The protein levels and antibodies had stabilized, and the myeloma was not progressing. And I wasn't dead. The doc said I didn't need any chemo right now. By this time, I had given up on wheatgrass, and for three months had been taking Spirulina. I started taking six tablets a day, but that didn't seem right, so I took ten per day. Ten made me feel stronger, less nervous, and I began to feel more relaxed. I was physically stronger.

I think the Spirulina was working because of its whole food aspects: The vitamin B complex, the proteins, the essential amino acids, and the chlorophyll. The rotten feeling I had in my body never came back after I started taking Spirulina. I started gaining weight back. I feel like a 25 year old, and I am 70! I think Spirulina cures and prevents cancer. It is a wonderful supplement for anything. Chlorophyll helps clean out the arteries, and Spirulina is very high in chlorophyll. It is grown in such intense sun. I felt so good about Spirulina that when a friend of ours for over twenty years began to have constant pain, I had to tell her about it.

This friend is 80 years old, the wife of a probate judge. She began to have constant pain in all her muscles and she couldn't sleep. She saw four different doctors, but they could not figure it out. Each time we saw her, she was worse. I told her she should take Spirulina, and about the story of taking ten tablets a day. She started taking the dosage. In one month she gained ten pounds. I asked her how she felt, and she said she felt young again.

She no longer sat with her arms folded up or walked hunched over. Her husband started taking Spirulina, and he feels much better too. I feel the Spirulina saved her from a lot of pain and made the quality of her life better.

One more health benefit from Spirulina: For ten years I was going to the Vitreoretinal Foundation in Tennessee for my eyes. I had a cataract removed ten years ago and had a retinal tear and laser treatment. Then three years ago I had a diagnosis of macular degeneration. I would see telephone polls with a crook in them. My center vision was faded. I had tunnel vision. The doctors said it could not be stopped; there is no cure.

During the time I had been taking Spirulina, and three years after the diagnosis, I had my eyes reexamined for a determination of the health of the retinal cells. The doctor looked it over and then he said, "Amazing! Your retina is not worse. In fact, it's better." I can now see poles with no center vision problems. I attribute the regeneration of my macular cells to Spirulina. *(David Schrieber, Keaau, HI)*

Testimonials from Around the World

Exhaustion/Energy

I have a 7:30 to 5 PM job. When I come home I still do my household chores, and still have time to spend with my three children aged 22, 19 and 17. Thanks to Spirulina I have so much more patience from not feeling exhausted anymore. I feel wonderful, energized, I feel l can handle anything; I just take four tablets in the morning and four in the afternoon. If it can help me in my serious condition, I am sure it can help others with all their complaints. Once again thank you Spirulina by Marcus Rohrer [Hawaiian]. *(Mrs. Latiff, Johannesburg, South Africa)*

Sports Training

I use Spirulina simply because it works and it is 100% natural. I feel fitter, have a better resistance and recover more quickly after exertion, whether it is a heavy training session or a match. My last condition test showed clearly that I had more stamina than last year. *(Erwin Koeman, Dutch National Soccer Team, Holland)*

Diabetes

I am a juvenile diabetic patient. After I have started taking Spirulina Pacifica [Hawaiian], I have found an amazing result. My fasting blood sugar count has come down from 294 mg to 120 mg. Thank you very much. *(Mohua Dasgupta, Kolkata, India)*

Digestion/Energy

Over the past year I have been taking Hawaiian Spirulina to neutralize some serious health problems. About four years ago I contracted acute and aggressive Ulcerative Colitis, necessitating the complete removal of my large intestine. In my particular case, this played havoc with my digestive system, especially in the area of essential nutrients.

During these last four years I have tried many health products and supplements and have had few permanent benefits. Most of these products helped for a short term, but were unable to sustain that on a continuing basis. Since discovering Hawaiian Spirulina, I have appreciated its benefits over an entire year. Its effects have not diminished, and I have found this to be a major source of my nutritional intake. Since taking Hawaiian Spirulina, I have felt myself being able to increase my energy levels and feel it has helped in my general lifestyle. *(Marie Cleanthous, St. Georges, South Australia)*

Feel Younger/Hair, Skin and Nails

I am 78 years of age and have been on Spirulina for over a year and find it highly beneficial. Since being on Marcus Rohrer Spirulina [Hawaiian], I have had no flu, my hair has stopped falling out and it is shiny and healthy. My nails are not cracking and they are healthy. My complexion, which was sallow, has become radiant. The tablets are pleasant to take. I am very active with lots of energy and feel like a man 20 years younger. I feel that this is largely due to Spirulina and I can highly recommend it. Thank you Spirulina! *(Bob Lipman, Cape Town, South Africa)*

Recovery from Operation

Last year I had to have a back operation. A big operation at my age, because at 62 you are not young any more. My surgeon advised me to take Marcus Rohrer Spirulina [Hawaiian] to help me get my strength back quickly. I must say – it was a golden tip! *(Mr. Verheyen, Lille, Belgium)*

Zest for Life

It was six months ago that my husband and I started taking the little green pills every morning, while the ongoing reaction from friends included remarks like "It's psychological" – "It's all in the mind" – "Impossible" – "Imagination." Now, these same friends are also experiencing the same zest for life thanks to

Marcus Rohrer Spirulina. *(S. Kotze, Kraaifontein, South Africa)*

"Physical Enrichment Without Being Rich"

I am not affluent and cannot afford a rich diet for my family. But Spirulina Pacifica [Hawaiian] has taken worries off me. Today with this Spirulina Pacifica every member of my family is physically enriched without being rich. Thank you Spirulina Pacifica. *(Indranath Mondal, Sonarpur, India)*

Weight Loss

Taking Spirulina by Marcus Rohrer, I easily managed to lose 15 pounds and I feel a lot fitter. I have a busy job as a representative and often felt tired and was overweight. I had tried everything, also homeopathic remedies, but nothing helped. I will certainly continue to use Spirulina. *(Mrs. Van Arendonk, Haarlem, The Netherlands)*

Spirulina Worked a Miracle for Me

I am an 83-year old lady living in my own in a flat. Last year I landed up in hospital after I fell one night and became very ill with bronchitis. When I was discharged I was very weak and frail. I was able to shuffle around with the aid of two crutches and only with extreme difficulty; I was so weak I wished that I would die. My daughter-in-law works in a pharmacy and she had heard all about Spirulina by Marcus Rohrer [Hawaiian]. She bought me a little bottle and after a few days I was truly amazed at the change in my condition. I have become more mobile and hardly need to use the crutches anymore. My blood pressure has never been so stable and I am certainly more alert. Several people have remarked on the improvement in my condition and are amazed at the change in me. I can only attribute this to the Spirulina and I want to thank you for this excellent product which has truly worked a miracle for me. *(Mrs. Stevens, Durban, South Africa)*

Energy/Endurance

I am a national level swimmer currently in the Australian Telstra Dolphins

Swim Team. I have been selected in the Australian Under 18 Team that competed in the Sydney Youth Olympics 2001.

I have only been using Spirulina for a short time but believe it has helped greatly with training and recovery. It gives me more energy and endurance. I recently swam a 2 km time trial with a 30 second personal best. *(David Cox, Beechboro, West Australia)*

Sports Training/Energy

I have been taking Marcus Rohrer Spirulina for over four years now. I have been participating in sports since I was 8. At age 12 I was training for football 5 times a week. I have been skateboarding for the past two years and I train very intensively. After being on my board for 5 to 6 hours I can feel every bone and muscle in my body. I then often take almost 20 Spirulina tablets and quickly feel energetic again. Spirulina has helped me a lot: Injuries like bruising and grazes heal really quickly and I am never troubled by growing pains. Before I go to school in the morning I often just drink water and take a handful of Spirulina. That keeps me fit all morning. *(Felix Nissen, 14 years old, Aurich, Germany)*

Appetite Suppressant/Healing after Operation

I think Spirulina by Marcus Rohrer is the miracle pill in the dark blue bottle. I had to have breast surgery in July and I wanted to be strong and healthy beforehand, so I took 6 pills a day. A week after my operation I had to go back to the plastic surgeon to see how I was healing. Well you would not believe what he said. He said that in all the years he has been in practice he has never seen anyone heal so quickly after an operation. My scars had closed completely and there were no complications. I put it all down to the effects Spirulina had on my body. I never get colds or flu and I have also got my husband on them. He was never a man for pills or vitamins and he swears by them. He tells all his friends about them.

Another reason why I use Spirulina is the fact that it actually reduces my appetite the natural way. I seldom feel hungry between meals. *(Mrs. J. Joaquim, Durban, South Africa)*

Energy

I study, work as a photo model and take part in sports often. Combining all this takes a lot of energy. Since I have been taking Spirulina by Marcus Rohrer, I have been able to cope easily with my active lifestyle.

To keep my energy level up I started to search for a supplement. Preferably something that was 100% natural. Friends advised me to try Marcus Rohrer Spirulina. A golden tip!

You do not notice the effects of Spirulina immediately. You must use it for a couple of weeks. Then you really notice the effects. For 18 months now I have been bursting with energy and can concentrate really well. Also, following a busy day modeling or studying I still have enough energy left to enjoy sport. Spirulina fits in perfectly with my lifestyle: Easy, natural and very effective. Really great! *(Charlotte van Zomeren, Amsterdam, Holland)*

Chronic Fatigue Syndrome

Hawaiian Spirulina! Have you heard of it? I would like to inform every person out there of this wonderful natural health food that comes in powder or tablet form.

Some years ago after running my swimwear shop alone for 13 years, I was completely exhausted and had chronic fatigue syndrome. I had to sell up and take two years out of my life trying to get better. Doctors can do nothing for you. My son had heard about Hawaiian Spirulina and bought some.

As each week went by I became stronger and happier and got into life again, my dark hair became shiny again, my nails grew stronger. I SWEAR BY SPIRULINA and have been taking it for 6 years now.

I look at the cost as a wonderful way to eat healthy. As I am now 61 years of age and want to always do the most with my life, I will always take Spirulina.

I have introduced it to all my family and friends and have watched them all sparkle with health and energy. Why don't you do yourself a favor also? *(Carol Prowse, Holloways Beach, Cairns, Australia)*

Olympic Swimmer

Spirulina gave me the recovery between sets to push even harder, improving my focus and boosting my immunity. It enabled me to fulfill the ultimate dream in any sportsman's life...The Olympics! I am greatly impressed with

Spirulina and from my experience there is no equal. Thank you Marcus Rohrer. *(Theo Verster, Olympic Swimmer, South Africa)*

Spirulina Brings Sunshine into my Life

When I take Marcus Rohrer Spirulina I notice that everything seems to become easier for me. I have more energy and life moves smoothly along. I am more cheerful and feel more optimistic about life. When I experience disappointments, I am better able to sort things out.

The benefits of Spirulina are most noticeable when one stops taking it. I then feel more tired and down in the dumps. Spirulina really brings sunshine into my life. *(Heidi G, 32 years old, Hoogstaten, Belgium)*

Blood Pressure and Blood Sugar

I am 63 years old and have been suffering from blood sugar and high blood pressure. Thank you for Spirulina Pacifica which has brought both sugar and pressure under control. Thank you again. *(T.P.V. Rao, Kolkata, India)*

Marathon and Triathlon Athlete

Real fitness is not about training – it's the speed of recovery after exercise that counts and determines one's level of fitness. Spirulina by Marcus Rohrer has been my helping hand through all my training and competing. It gives me the recovery time and fitness that I need. *(Nick Bester, professional Ultra Marathon and Triathlon athlete, South Africa)*

BIBLIOGRAPHY

Ayehunie, S., Belay, A., Baba, T.W., and Ruprecht, R.M. (May 1, 1998). "Inhibition of HIV1 replication by an aqueous extract of Spirulina platensis (Arthrospira platensis)." *J Acquir Immune Defic. Syndr. Hum. Retroviro,* 18(1):7-12.

Becker, E. W., B. Jakober, D. Luft, and R.-M. Schmulling. (1986) "Clinical and Biochemical Evaluations of the Alga Spirulina with Regard to Its Application in the Treatment of Obesity." *Nutrition Reports International,* Vol. 33, No.4.

Belch, J. J. F., D. Ansell, R. Madhok, and R. D. Sturrock (1988). "The effects of altering dietary essential fatty acids on requirements for non-steroidal anti-inflammatory drugs in patients with rheumatoid arthritis: a double-blind placebo controlled study." *Annals of the Rheumatic Diseases,* 47:96-104.

Ben-Amotz, Ami, Shoshana Mokady, Samuel Edelstein, and Mordhay Avron (July 1989). "Bioavailability of a Natural Isomer Mixture as Compared with Synthetic all-trans-Beta-Carotene in Rats and Chicks." *Journal of Nutrition,* Vol. 119, No.7.

Bendich, Adrianne (1988). "A Role for Carotenoids in Immune Function." *Clinical Nutrition,* Vol. 7, 113-117.

Blinkova, L.P., Gorobets, O.B., and Baturo, A.P. (March-April 2001). "Biological activity of Spirulina." *Zh Mikrobiol Epidemiol Immunobiol,* (2):114-8.

Boyd, M. R. et al (1989). "AIDS anti-viral sulfolipids from cyanobacteria (blue-green alga)." *Journal of the National Cancer Institute,* 81 (16) 1254.

Brevard, Patricia B. (1989). "Beta-carotene affects white blood cells in human peripheral blood." *Nutrition Reports International,* Vol. 40, No. 1.

Bruce, Gene (May 1988). "The Myth of Vegetarian B-12." East West Journal.

Buletsa, B.A., Ihnatovych II, Lupych, P.P., and Pulyk, O.R. (Oct.-Dec. 1996). "The prevalence, structure and clinical problems of multiple sclerosis in the Transcarpathian area based on epidemiological study data." *Lik Sprava.,* (10-12):163-5.

Challem, Jack Joseph (1981). *Spirulina: What It Is... The Health Benefits It Can Give You.* Keats Publishing Inc., New Canaan, CT.

Chamorro, G., Salazar, M., Araujo, K.G., dos Santos C.P., Ceballos, G., and Castillo, L.F. (Sept. 2002). "Update on the pharmacology of Spirulina (Arthrospira), an unconventional food." *Arch Latinoam Nutr.,* 52(3):232-40.

Coutsoudis, A., P. Keipiela, H. Coovadia, et al (1992). "Vitamin A supplementation enhances specific IgC antibody levels and total lymphocyte numbers while improving morbidity in measles." *Pediatric Infectious Disease,* 1:203-209.

Crisafi, Daniel J. (November/December 1992). "Gamma-linolenic acid, a vital nutrient." *Health Naturally.*

Cysewski, Gerald R. (1992). "Ocean-Chill Drying of Microalgae and Microalgal Products." Patent proposal.

Dasgupta, T., Banejee, S., Yadav, P.K., and Rao, A.R. (Oct. 2001). "Chemomodulation of carcinogen metabolizing enzymes, antioxidant profiles and skin and forestomach papillomagenesis by Spirulina platensis." *Mol Cell Biochem.,* 226(1-2):27-38.

Diaz del Calstillo, Bernal (1956). *The Discovery and Conquest of Mexico 1517-1521.* Farrar, Straus, and Cudahy.

Doll, R. and R. Peto (1981). "The causes of cancer: quantitative estimates of avoidable risks of cancer in the United States today." *Journal of National Cancer Institute*, 66:1191-1308.

Dunne, Lavon J. (1990). Nutrition Almanac, Third Edition. McGraw-Hill.

Fox, Ripley D. (February 1985). "Spirulina, The Alga That Can End Malnutrition." *The Futurist*.

Fox, Ripley D. (1987). "Spirulina, real aid to development." In *Twelfth International Seaweed Symposium*, edited by M.A. Ragan and C.J. Bird. *Hydrobiologia*, 151/152:95-97.

Frieden, T., A. Sowell, K. Henning, et al (1992). "Vitamin A levels and severity of measles." *American Journal of Diseases of Children*, 146: 182-186.

Furst, Peter T. (1978). "Spirulina." *Human Nature*, 60.

Garewal, H., N. Ampel, R. Watson, et al (1992). "A preliminary trial of beta-carotene in subjects infected with the human immunodeficiency virus." *Journal of Nutrition*, 122:728-732.

Gemma, C., Meshes, M.H., Sepesi, B., Choo, K., Holmes, D.B., and Bickford, P.C. (July 15, 2002). "Diets enriched in foods with high antioxidant activity reverse age-induced decreases in cerebellar beta-adrenergic function and increases in proinflammatory cytokines." *J Nerosci.*, 22(14):6114-20.

Gorban', E.M., Orynchak, M.A., Virstiuk, N.G., Kuprash, L.P., Panteleimonova, T.M., and Sharabura, L.B. (Sept. 2000). "Clinical and experimental study of spirulina efficacy in chronic diffuse liver diseases." *Lik Sprava.*, (6):89-93.

Hayashi, K., Hayashi, T., and Kojima, I. (Oct. 10, 1996). "A natural sulfated polysaccharide, calcium spirulan, isolated from Spirulina platensis: in vitro and ex vivo evaluation of anti-herpes simplex virus and anti-human immunodeficiency virus activities." AIDS Res. Hum. Retroviruses, 12(15):1463-71.

Hayashi, O., Katoh, T., and Okuwaki, Y. (Oct. 1994). "Enhancement of antibody production in mice by dietary Spirulina platensis." *J. Nutr. Sci. Vitaminol (Tokyo)*, 40(5):431-41.

Hayashi, T., Hayashi, K., Maeda, M., and Kojima, I. (Jan 1996). "Calcium spirulan, an inhibitor of enveloped virus replication, from blue-green alga Spirulina platensis." *J. Nat. Prod.*, 59(1):83-7.

Health Media of America (1991-1992). *The Nutrition Report*, Vols. 9 and 10.

Henrikson, Robert (1989). *Earth Food Spirulina*. Laguna Beach, CA: Ronore Enterprises, Inc.

Hernandez-Corona, A., Nieves, I., Meckes, M., Chamorro, G., and Barron, B.L. (Dec. 2002). "Antiviral activity of Spirulina maxima against herpes simplex virus type 2." *Antiviral Res.*, 56(3):279-85.

Hirahashi, T., Matsumoto, M., Hazeki, K., Saeki, Y., Ui, M., and Seya, T. (Mar. 2002). "Activation of the human innate immune system by Spirulina: augmentation of interferon production and NK cytotoxicity by oral administration of hot water extract of Spirulina platensis." Int. *Immunopharmacol.*, 2(4):423-34.

Horrobin, D. F. (1983). "The role of essential fatty acids and prostaglandins in the premenstrual syndrome." *Journal of Reproductive Medicine*, 28:465-468.

Howard, Saundra (1982). The Spirulina Diet. Secaucus, NJ: Lyle Stuart Inc.

Iijima, N., I. Fugii, H. Shimamatsu, and S. Katoh. "Anti-tumor agent and method of treatment therewith." U.S. Patent Pending, Ref. No. P1150-726-A82679.

Iwata, K., Inayama, T., and Kato, T. (April 1990). "Effects of Spirulina platensis on plasma lipoprotein lipase activity in fructose-induced hyperlipidemic rats." *J. Nutr. Sci. Vitaminol (Tokyo)*, 36(2):165-71.

Jian, L., Du, C.J., Lee, A.H., and Binns, C.W. (Mar. 1, 2005). "Do dietary lycopene and other carotenoids protect against prostate cancer?" *Int. J. Cancer*, 113(6):1010-4.

Johns Hopkins University (1991). "Food for the Heart." *The Johns Hopkins Medical Letter*, Vol. 2, No.12.

Kapoor, R. and Mehta, U. (Jan. 1993). "Effect of supplementation of blue green alga (Spirulina) on outcome of pregnancy in rats." *Plant Foods Hum. Nutr.*, 43(1):29-35.

Kapoor, R. and Mehta, U. (1998). "Supplementary effect of spirulina on hematological status of rats during pregnancy and lactation." *Plant Foods Hum. Nutr.*, 52(4):315-24.

Karpov, L.M., Brown II, Poltavtseva, N.V., Ershova, O.N., Karakis, S.G., Vasil'eva, T.V., and Chaban luL. (May-June 2000). "The postradiation use of vitamin-containing complexes and a phycocyanin extract in a radiation lesion in rats." *Radiats Biol Radioecol.*, 40(3):310-4.

Keithley, E.M., Canto, C., Zheng, Q.Y., Wang, X., Fischel-Ghodsian, N., and Johnson, K.R. (July 28, 2005). "Cu/Zn superoxide dismutase and age-related hearing loss." *Hear Res.*

Kendler, Barry S. (1987). "Gamma-linolenic-acid: physiological effects and potential medical applications." *Journal of Applied Nutrition*, Vol. 39, No.2.

Kim, H.M., Lee, E.H., Cho, H.H., and Moon, Y.H. (April 1, 1998). "Inhibitory effect of mast cell-mediated immediate-type allergic reactions in rats by spirulina." *Biochem Pharmacol*, 55(7):1071-6.

Kinnula, V.L. (Aug. 2005). "Focus on antioxidant enzymes and antioxidant strategies in smoking related airway diseases." *Thorax*, 60(8):693-700

Kornhauser, A., W. Wamer, and A. Giles, Jr. (1986). "Protective effects of beta-carotene against psoralen phototoxicity: relevance to protection against carcinogenesis." *Antimutagenesis and Anticarcinogenesis Mechanisms*, edited by D. M. Shankel, P.E. Hartman, T. Kado Plenum Press.

Kowald, A., Lehrach, H., and Klipp, E. (Aug. 5, 2005). "Alternative pathways as mechanism for the negative effects associated with overexpression of superoxide dismutase." J. Theor. Biol.

Mao, T.K., Van de Water, J., and Gershwin, M.E. (Spring 2005). "Effects of Spirulina-based dietary supplement on cytokine production from allergic rhinitis patients." *J. Med. Food*, 8(1):27-30.

Mathew, B., Sankaranarayanan, R., Nair, P.P., Varghese, C., Somanathan, T., Amma, B.P., Amma, N.S., and Nair, M.K. (1995). "Evaluation of chemoprevention of oral cancer with Spirulina fusiformis." *Nutr. Cancer*, 24(2):197-202.

Mathews-Roth, Micheline M. (1981). "Carotenoids in Medical Applications." *Carotenoids as Colorants and Vitamin A Precursors*, edited by J.C. Bauernfeind. Academic Press.

Michka (1990). *La Spiruline, L'homme et la planète*. Geneva: Terra Magna.

Mishima, T., Murata, J., Toyoshima, M., Fujii, H., Nakajima, M., Hayashi, T., Kato, T., and Saiki, I. (Aug. 1998). "Inhibition of tumor invasion and metastasis by calcium spirulan (Ca-SP), a novel sulfated polysaccharide derived from blue-green alga, Spirulina patensis." *Clin. Exp. Metastasis*, 16(6):541-50.

Morcos NC., M Bems, and WL. Henry. 1988. Phycocyanin: laser activation, cytotoxic effects, and uptake in human atherosclerotic plaque. *Lasers Surg Med.* 8(1): 10-7

National Research Council (1989). Diet and Health: *Implications for Reducing Chronic Disease Risk*. National Academy Press, Washington, D.C.

Nayaka, N. et al (June 1988). "Cholesterol lowering effects of Spirulina." *Nutrition Reports International*, Vol. 37, No.6.

Nozik-Grayck, E., Suliman, H.B., and Piantadosi, C.A. (Aug. 5, 2005). "Extracellular superoxide dismutase." *Int. J. Biochem Cell Biol.*

Otles, S. and Pire, R. (Nov.-Dec. 2001). "Fatty acid composition of Chlorella and Spirulina microalgae species." *J. AOAC Int.*, 84(6):1708-14.

Palan, Prabhudas R., Magdy S. Mikhail, Jayasri Basu, and Seymour L. Romney (1992). "B-Carotene levels in exfoliated cervicovaginal epithelial cells in cervical intraepithelial neoplasia and cervical cancer." *American Journal of Obstetrics and Gynecology*, 167:1899-1903.

Pinero Estrada, J.E., Bermejo Bescos, P., and Villar del Fresno, A.M. (May-July 2001). "Antioxidant activity of different fractions of Spirulina platensis protean extract." *Farmco*, 56(5-7):497-500.

Pong, K. (Feb. 2003). "Oxidative stress in neurodegenerative diseases: therapeutic implications for superoxide dismutase mimetics." *Expert Opinion Biol. Ther.*, 3(1):127-39.

Pugh, N., Ross, S.A., ElSohly, H.N., ElSohly, M.A., and Pasco, D.S. (Nov. 2001). "Isolation of three high molecular weight polysaccharide preparations with potent immunostimulatory activity from Spirulina platensis, aphanizomenon flos-aquae and Chlorella pyrenoidosa." *Planta Med.*, 67(8):737-42.

Qureshi, M.A. and Ali, R.A. (Aug. 1996). "Spirulina platensis exposure enhances macrophage phagocytic function in cats." *Immunopharmacol Immunotoxicol*, 18(3):457-63.

Qureshi, M.A., Garlich, J.D., and Kidd, M.T. (Aug. 1996). "Dietary Spirulina platensis enhances humoral and cell-mediated immune functions in chickens." *Immunopharmacol Immunotoxicol*, 18(3):465-76.

Reddy, C.M., Bhat, V.B., Kiranmai, G., Reddy, M.N., Reddanna, P., and Madyastha, K.M. (Nov. 2, 2000). "Selective inhibition of cyclooxygenase-2 by C-phycocyanin, a biliprotein from Spirulina platensis." Biochem Biophys. *Res. Commun.*, 277(3):599-603.

Remirez, D., Gonzalez, R., Merino, N., Rodriguez, S., and Ancheta, O. (April 2002). "Inhibitory effects of Spirulina in zymosan-induced arthritis in mice." *Mediators Inflamm.*, 11(2):75-9.

Remirez, D., Ledon, N., and Gonzalez R. (April 2002). "Role of histamine in the inhibitory effects of phycocyanin in experimental models of allergic inflammatory response." *Mediators Imflamm.*, 11(2):81-5.

Renke, J., Szlagatys-Sidorkiewicz, A., Popadiuk, S., Korzon, M., Bugajczyk, B., Szumera, M., and Wozniak, M. (Apr.-June 2005). "Superoxide dismutase in children with juvenile idiopathic arthritis." *Med. Wieku Rozwoj (Poland)*, 9(2):205-12.

Ribaya-Mercado, J.D. and Blumberg J.B. (Dec. 2004). "Lutein and zeaxanthin and their potential roles in disease prevention." *J. Am. Coll. Nutr.*, 23(6Suppl):567S-587S.

Richmond, Amos (1990). "Large scale microalgal culture and applications." Progress in *Phycological Research*, Vol. 7, edited by Round and Chapman. Biopress Ltd.

Richmond, Amos (1988). "Spirulina." *Micro-Algal Biotechnology*, edited by Michael A. and Lesley J. Borowitska. Cambridge University Press.

Rodriguez-Hernandez, A., Ble-Castillo, J.L., Juarez-Oropeza, M.A., and Diaz-Zagoya, J.C. (July 20, 2001). "Spirulina maxima prevents fatty liver formation in CD-1 male and female mice with experimental diabetes." *Life Sci.*, 69(9):1029-37.

Romay, C., Ledon, N., and Gonzalez, R. (Dec. 2000). "Effects of phycocyanin extract on prostaglandin E2 levels in mouse ear inflammation test." *Arzneimittelforschung (Cuba)*, 50(12):1106-9.

Romay, C.H., Gonzalez, R., Ledon, N., Remirez, D., and Rimbau, V. (June 2003). "C-phycocyanin: a biliprotein with antioxidant, anti-inflammatory and neuroprotective effects." Curr. Protein Pept Sci., 4(3):207-16.

Samuels, R., Mani, U.V., Iyer, U.M., and Nayak, U.S. (Summer 2002). "Hypocholesterolemic effect of spirulina in patients with hyperlipidemic nephritic syndrome." *J. Med. Food*, 5(2):91-6.

Sautier C. and J. Tremolieres (1976). "Food value of Spirulina in humans." *Ann. Nutrition Alim.*, 30:517-534.

Schwartz, Joel, Gerald Shklar, Susan Reid, and Diane Trickier (1988). "Prevention of Experimental Oral Cancer by Extracts of Spirulina-Dunaliella Algae." *Nutrition and Cancer*, Vol. II, No.2

Shimidzu N., M. Goto, and W. Miki. 1996. Carotenoids as singlet oxygen quenchers in marine organisms. *Fisheries Science.* 62(1): 134-137.

Stahelin, H. B., K. F. Gey, M. Eicholzer, and E. Ludin (1991). "B-Carotene and cancer prevention: the Basel Study." *American Journal of Clinical Nutrition,* 53: 265S-9S.

Stahl, W., and Sies, H. (May 30, 2005). "Bioactivity and protective effects of natural carotenoids." *Biochem Biophys Acta,* 1740(2):101-7.

Stich, H., B. Mathew, R. Sankaranarayanan, et al (1991). "Remission of oral precancerous lesions of tobacco/areca nut chewers following administration of beta carotene or vitamin A, and maintenance of the protective effect." Cancer Detection, 15:93-98.

Switzer, Larry (1982). Spirulina, *The Whole Food Revolution.* New York: Bantam Books.

Teas, J., Herbert, J.R., Fitton, J.H., and Zimba P.V. (2004). "Algae-a poor man's HAART?" *Med Hypotheses,* 62(4):507-10.

Torres-Duran, P.V., Miranda-Zamora, R., Paredes-Carbajal, M.C., Mascher, D., Diaz-Zagoya, J.C., and Juarez-Oropeza, M.A. (April 1998). "Spirulina maxima prevents induction of fatty liver by carbon tetrachloride in the rat." *Biochem Mol. Biol. Int.,* 44(4):787-93.

Van Herpen-Broekmans, W.M., Klopping-Ketelaars, I.A., Bots, M.L., Kluft, C., Princen, H., Hendriks, H.F., Tijburg, L.B., van Poppel, G., and Kardinaal, A.F. (2004). "Serum carotenoids and vitamins in relation to markers of endothelial function and inflammation." *Eur. J. Epidemiol,* 19(10):915-21.

Wald, N. J., S. G. Thompson, J. W. Densem, J. Boreham, and A. Bailey (1988). "Serum beta-carotene and subsequent risk of cancer: Results from the BUPA Study." *British Journal of Cancer,* 57:428-433.

Wang, J., Chang, C.F., Chou, J., Chen, H.L., Deng, X., Harvey, B.K., Cadet, J.L., and Bickford, P.C. (May 2005). "Dietary supplementation with blueberries, spinach, or spirulina reduces ischemic brain damage." *Exp. Neurol.,* 193(1):75-84.

Wolf, George (1992). "Retinoids and carotenoids as inhibitors of carcinogenesis and inducers of cell-cell communication." *Nutrition Reviews,* Vol. 50, No.9.

Wu, L.C., Ho, J.A., Shieh, M.C., and Lu, I.W. (May 18, 2005). "Antioxidant and antiproliferative activities of Spirulina and Chlorella water extracts." *J. Agric Food Chem.,* 53(10):4207-12.

Wynder, E. L. and G. B. Gori (1977). "Contribution of the environment to cancer incidence: an epidemiologic exercise." *Journal of National Cancer Institute,* 58:825-832.

Zhang, H.Q., Lin, A.P., Sun, Y., and Deng, Y.M. (Dec. 2001). "Chemo- and radio-protective effects of polysaccharide of Spirulina platensis on hemopoietic system of mice and dogs." *Acta Pharmacol. Sin.,* 22(12):1121-4.

Ziboh, Vincent A. and Mark P. Fletcher (1992). "Dose-response effects of dietary gamma linolenic acid-enriched oils on human polymorphonuclear-neutrophil biosynthesis of leukotriene B4." *American Journal of Clinical Nutrition,* 55:39-45.

Ziegler, R.G. (1989). "A review of epidemiologic evidence that carotenoids reduce the risk of cancer." *Journal of Nutrition,* 119:116-122.

ABOUT THE AUTHORS

Kelly Moorhead has been studying and growing Spirulina for over twenty years. Schooled in Marine Biology at the University of California, Kelly was responsible for Spirulina cultivation and production with the Marine Science Institute of University of California at Santa Barbara and later with Hawaii's Oceanic Institute.

Kelly spent the next twenty years of his career at Cyanotech where he devoted himself to studying, developing, producing and marketing Hawaiian Spirulina and Natural Astaxanthin. Kelly passed away in 2004.

Bob Capelli has been involved in natural healing and herbology for almost twenty years. After graduating from Rutgers University with a degree in liberal arts, Bob spent four years traveling and working in developing countries in Asia and South America, where he learned about and developed a deep respect for the medicinal power of plants. Upon returning to the United States Bob began working in the natural supplement industry where he has remained for the last fifteen years. Bob realized his dream job four years ago when he joined Cyanotech, allowing him to work with the premier producers of Spirulina and Natural Astaxanthin from microalgae.

Dr. Gerald Cysewski is recognized as a world authority on microalgae. He has over thirty years experience in microalgae research and commercial production of microalgae products. His work on microalgae in 1976 was supported by the National Science Foundation at the University of California at Santa Barbara where he was an assistant professor in the department of Chemical & Nuclear Engineering He carried on his work at Battelle Northwest as group leader of microalgae research.

Dr. Cysewski co-founded Cyanotech Corporation in 1983 in Washington State. He initially served as the Company's Scientific Director and became President and CEO of Cyanotech in 1990. As the Company's Scientific Director he sought the optimum site to launch commercial production of microalgae and found the Kona coast of Hawaii, a region with abundant sunlight virtually year-round, a ready source of pure water from island aquifers, deep-ocean seawater nearby to fuel a new chill-drying technology, and access to transportation and skilled labor. Cyanotech's location combined with its advanced technology has made it the premier producer of microalgae in the world.

Dr. Cysewski holds a Bachelor of Science in Chemical Engineering from the University of Washington and a Doctorate in Chemical Engineering from the University of California at Berkeley.